This book is dedicated
to the dual memory of Michel de Brunhoff,
Editor in Chief of the French edition of *Vogue*,
and his son Pascal de Brunhoff, Parisian student,
who in his twentieth year was shot by the Nazis.

Edmonde Charles-Roux

CHANEL
and her world

Friends, Fashion, and Fame

The Vendome Press

New York

VOGUE

CONFIRMATION DE
LA MODE · RIVIERA
JANVIER 1932
PRIX 6 FRANCS

"Someone suggested to an author I know, regarding a book of his that was about to appear and whose heroine could be recognized only too readily, that, even then, he change at least the color of her hair. If blond, she might not, it would seem, betray the identity of a woman who is dark-haired. Well, I do not find that childish, I find it scandalous. I continue to insist upon naming names, to find interesting only those books that are left open like swinging doors, books for which one does not have to find a key. Fortunately, the days of romantically contrived literature are numbered."

André Breton, *Nadja*

". . . I do not allow that you have the right of life or death over pseudo-human beings, sprung armed or disarmed from your whims. Restrict yourself to giving me your memoirs. Let me know the real names, and prove to me that you have in no way tampered with your heroes."

André Breton, *Point du jour*

Riviera.
Cover of French *Vogue*,
January 1932. Bibliothèque
des Arts Décoratifs, Paris.

Mademoiselle
Chanel. Drawing
by Drian.

Chanel, who always seemed so utterly of our time, actually came from another century, having been born in 1883. In that year, President Chester Alan Arthur inaugurated a work of engineering then regarded as the ultimate in daring, the Brooklyn Bridge; in Moscow, Tsar Alexander II and his Tsaritsa, more bedecked than idols (she under some thirty-two kilos of silver fabric), were crowned Emperor and Empress of all the Russias; in Paris, news arrived that the French flag had just been raised over the citadel of Hanoi; in Berlin, vindictive articles, signed by Bismarck, proclaimed that France was decidedly a nation of madmen; and in London, the subjects of austere Queen Victoria asked themselves whether Her Majesty could have been in love with her manservant. Deeply affected by the death of John Brown, the elderly monarch canceled all audiences. No newspaper, however, made note of the fact that in a hospital deep within provincial France a second child had been born to a poor, unmarried couple. The father was a small-wares peddler from the Cévennes, the mother a peasant of stock native to the Auvergne, and the newborn a little girl named Gabrielle Chanel. In her own way, she too would reign, rule, and govern.

Why was it that, having completely escaped the absurdities of the fashion world, Mademoiselle Chanel would to the end of her days strive relentlessly to conceal her personal origins? The father of Chanel, if one believed what she said, was a man of mystery, who fathered more children than he could feed, spent more than he earned, and finally disappeared. But how did he make a living? To this question Chanel never gave a reply. We shall never know why Gabrielle Chanel adopted such reticence in regard to her family—her several brothers, her mother whose early death left little Gabrielle to the mercies of a provincial orphanage.

The story of Chanel is difficult to tell. She did not even experience what most women of her generation did—marriage and children. Abandoned by her father the week after her mother died, Gabrielle the child suffered all the harshness of convent life, by which we do not mean misery and maltreatment but, rather, strictness, solitude, and mental anguish.

Then came problematic beginnings.

What could be hoped, at that time, for a poor girl brought up by the charity of nuns? Gabrielle risked, while barely out of adolescence, finding herself placed as a clerk with some regional tradesman. This was what she had to resist, had to escape. At age eighteen, she already had no other thought. Still, the young Chanel made her start in Moulins with just such an employment, working for a shopkeeper specializing in layettes, linens, and small wares.

Several years passed, filled mainly with false starts. Among these was a move to Vichy, where, dreaming of a career in the theatre, she made a stab at singing and even dancing.

Chanel was twenty-five when she met the scion of a high bourgeois family, who proposed, not marriage but a life together. This was Étienne Balsan, a gentleman horse breeder and riding enthusiast. Chanel accepted and moved in with him near Paris. Now began an apprenticeship that would reveal to her both the charms of château life and the secrets of the role that had devolved upon her: She was succeeding the celebrated courtesan Émilienne d'Alençon as the chatelain's official mistress.

One can imagine the exasperation of Gabrielle Chanel in later years whenever she read the legends that had her leaving her native province attired in a cotton apron and sabots. No doubt she was put together in a simple manner, but it is certain that upon her arrival in Paris in 1909, Chanel was already dressed according to her own taste—that is, like no

Portrait of Chanel
by Jean Cocteau.

one else—and possessed of the vibrant inner quality that would make her unforgettable to everyone she met.

Now commenced a whimsical period during which Chanel drank deeply of whatever the cup of life offered. She became both an equestrienne and a seductress, exercising the best horses then available in France and exploiting the assets that were peculiarly her own: great natural beauty and a rare charm. Seen everywhere—Paris, Pau, Cannes, Deauville—Chanel emerged as the darling of all the young lions of the age. After Balsan came "Boy" Capel, a brilliantly intelligent Englishman and her greatest—possibly her only—love. But he too merely made Chanel his mistress, without there ever being the possibility of marriage.

Happy? Gabrielle Chanel pretended that she was, although many years later she would admit, in rare, unguarded moments, that this was a time, more than ever afterward, when she often found herself in tears. She also professed to have had only modest aspirations, wanting true love, to be chosen, preferred, and that the choice be for always. But destiny decreed that such happiness would never be hers.

In the summer of 1913 Chanel decided to break with the life of a kept woman and all the vexations it entailed. Thus, with the financial help of Boy Capel, she settled in Deauville and opened her first boutique. She entered into the business with drums beating, as if, by the weight of her own body, she could force open the door to freedom.

Nothing thereafter would make Chanel give up an activity that, however much it may have originated as merely a means of taking revenge upon life, soon became her whole raison d'être. And nothing could stop her, not even the war that exploded within a year, nor yet the rumble of cannons sounding all the way from Verdun. Once she began to apply herself, Chanel became a *femme d'entreprise* forever. Throughout the remainder of her life

Coco Chanel
in her apartment at
the Ritz. Photo by
François Kollar for
Harper's Bazaar.
Paris, 1937.

she would work unremittingly as both craftsman and businesswoman, imposing her personal conception of the art of dressing upon an ever-expanding clientele. Along the way she crossed swords with the greatest couturier of the age, Paul Poiret, luring away his customers one by one and recruiting them into the band of women who, on her orders, gave up aigrettes, long hair, and hobble skirts.

In the postwar era, beginning in 1918, and then again in the prewar period of the thirties, Chanel received the attentions of high-born, aristocratic suitors. The first was the extraordinarily handsome, but ruined and exiled, Grand Duke Dimitri of Russia; the second the fabulously rich and powerful Duke of Westminster. In her own way, Chanel derived real benefits from these liaisons. With the Russian she developed a taste for warm, fur-lined coats and for fabrics of almost Byzantine opulence, while through the Englishman she fell in love with British tweeds, which she had women wear with jersey blouses and ropes of pearls, a revolutionary combination at the time. She also acquired the English respect for comfort, and never again allowed that luxury could have any purpose other than to make simplicity appear remarkable.

Chanel never resisted the association of her name with those of the two aristocrats, which, however, cannot be construed to mean that these were the men to whom she felt the most attached. Her heart concealed other memories, other long-lost loves, other sorrows, and once she had determined that a name should not be mentioned, never again would a syllable of it pass her lips.

Then came another war and the French defeat. In occupied Paris the sound of German boots made the benign fashion parade over which Chanel presided seem totally frivolous. Thus, she demobilized her battalion of mannequins and the next morning closed the House

Mademoiselle Chanel
in her apartment
at the Ritz. Drawing
by Christian Bérard.

of Chanel. For this action Chanel suffered unsparing criticism, with the fashion industry accusing her of desertion. She could not have cared less.

The Occupation proved to be a very dark moment in the life of Chanel. Her affair with a German officer, although discreetly conducted, created a scandal as soon as it was known and then brought violent recriminations once the war was over.

Peace returned, but prewar France had ceased to exist. No one was more conscious of this than Gabrielle Chanel. Where, for instance, were the millionaires of old? The foreign women who formerly came to Paris and bought dresses by the dozen? Chanel did not reopen her salon. Withdrawn into herself and self-exiled to Switzerland, she watched with peasant shrewdness and kept quiet. This inactivity continued for a full decade.

Paris quickly forgets. Soon no one spoke of Chanel, and a new public knew her merely as a name. As for Chanel, only the rising star of a very great couturier could revive the old sense of competition. But Christian Dior at his zenith promised to be a worthy adversary. In 1954 Chanel set out to destroy him as if it were a holy mission. In this she did not succeed, but managed, in her lightning reappearance, to challenge him quite seriously. Indeed, Chanel realized a new and immense success. Thus did this indomitable woman, now seventy-one years old, rediscover the old passion for her métier. She worked with a ferocious dedication—as well as with utter indifference to the emotional disarray caused by her demands and rages. Whenever these rang out, the life of a building with several stories and a staff of hundreds remained suspended as if from her fingers or from the very sound of her voice.

It was quite something to live with Chanel those days and nights prior to the first showing of each new collection. And to see her exhausted, having consumed nothing since morning but a glass of water, yet still hard at it because forever unsatisfied. So exalted was her idea of perfection that she could tolerate none of the compromises that are the stock-in-trade of others. It was also quite something to hear "Mademoiselle," her mouth full of invective, launch into one of the soliloquies that with her passed for conversation and that accompanied her battle with thread, wool, fabric, the difficult shape, or anything else that resisted her.

How many nights, how many days did Chanel spend in this way during her long life? Was it really necessary to go to such lengths in order to be, in the eyes of the world, the great Chanel?

Chanel lived at the very center of an extraordinary professional success; yet she suffered extreme loneliness, having failed in what meant the most to her—the life of a woman. What she had, however, was more independence, more freedom than most could ever imagine.

Her fate stands in contradiction to the thesis that equality between the sexes is the determining condition of female happiness. As a business executive, Chanel proved to be altogether the equal of men, often their superior, but in her private life she was the most vulnerable of women. The worst of it was that while fashion may have constituted the focus of her entire existence, this grand preoccupation could not satisfy her need for love, a realm in which Gabrielle Chanel met nothing but disillusionment.

Occasionally, at the end of her strength, Chanel could be heard saying to herself "Ah! I shall die of this." One's heart went out to her. After all, to die for an armhole, for a braid positioned a bit higher or lower, to perish for a certain idea of elegance—did this not take it a bit too far? But the battle went on and on, as long as Chanel had a breath left in her.

It was at the end of a week in which she may have thought more often than usual, "Ah! I shall die of this," that Gabrielle Chanel breathed no more. The 10th of June 1971 fell on Sunday, the day of rest. When her heart stopped, the great woman was eighty-seven years old. Her reign over the world of fashion had endured almost half a century.

EDMONDE CHARLES-ROUX

"Fashion does not only exist in dresses;
fashion is in the air, it is brought in by the wind,
one feels it coming, breathes it in,
it is in the sky and on the pavement,
it depends on ideas, customs, and happenings."
Coco Chanel

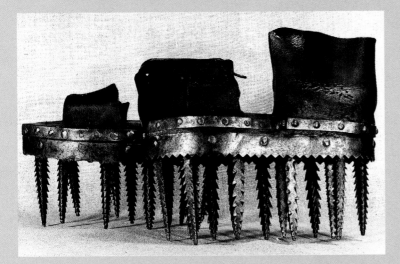

In the Cévennes chestnut groves

This hamlet in the Cévennes was the geographic cradle of the Chanel family. But not even in her most candid and confidential moments would Gabrielle Chanel, that otherwise courageous and liberated woman, ever have admitted that her ancestors came from Ponteils. Like all the inhabitants of the hamlet, the Chanels were originally rural folk with scarcely any land, hiring out to gather chestnuts and living almost exclusively by this means—well or badly depending on the harvest. At the beginning of the 19th century the great-grandfather of Gabrielle made a marriage that permitted him to give up day labor and stop breaking his back for others. Using his wife's very modest dowry, he rented a hall and there opened a tavern. Today the local people still say *"le Chanel"* when referring to the farmhouse that once sheltered the family bistro of Ponteils.

Ponteils, a lost hamlet

The primitive dwellings of the Cévennes have resisted time, winter cold, rural exodus, even abandonment. But while their roofs sag dangerously, the massive rustic houses speak of times when rural civilization was at its zenith. Then came the collapse.

△◁ "Sawtooth" shoes, once used by the peasants of the Cévennes to shell chestnuts fallen to the ground. Musée des Arts et Traditions, Paris.

△ The *trulli* of Apulia? Sardinian *nouraghe*? No, the streetlike courtyard and outbuildings of *le Chanel*.

◁ Ponteils today, with its great chestnut tree and what remains of *le Chanel*.

In 1850, two different diseases struck the chestnut groves, bringing poverty, which in turn emptied Ponteils of its inhabitants. The sons of the tavern keeper left the Cévennes, and the man who would be the grandfather of Gabrielle Chanel became a peddler, an itinerant small-wares salesman. While making the rounds of markets and fairs in both towns and cities, he married a girl already pregnant by him. Their son, the father of Gabrielle, was born at Nîmes and would follow in his father's trade.

◁ An arch leads to the cellar of this economical and carefully organized dwelling, a functional farmhouse providing a good volume of enclosed space for all the necessities of daily life.

△ Painted sheet-metal sign, early 19th century. Musée Fontenelle-Mondress, Thiers. The *mercelot*, a traveling peddler who, in addition to his *mercerie* ("small wares"), also sold almanacs.

The decline of rural France

Over a century and a half have passed since the great-grandfather of Gabrielle Chanel served as tavern keeper in this simple, primitive, and virtually unchanged Cévenole farmhouse, using as his public room an out-building space rented from a small landholder. The

appearance of a village café marked the true turning point in the mores of the rural world. By relieving isolation, it also ruptured the unity of family life, and affected many other traditions and customs, such as evenings at home before the fire. Now the men who remained in Ponteils gathered every night in the bistro. But even these were old men, for the city had claimed the younger ones. Such was the general trend during the 1850–80 period, and the descendants of tavern-keeper Chanel were no exception. Both his son and his grandson became itinerant peddlers, and both fathered children by women they had not married. It was to the younger couple—to the *mercelot* father—that Gabrielle Chanel was born in 1883. Ponteils, a bastion of the peasant spirit, really discloses the most about the bold and indomitable couturière.

△ The "common" or family room so essential to peasant life. Its "décor" is typical of taverns during the period when rural France went into decline with the flight of the peasantry to the city.

In Saumur it was still Second Empire

Saumur, a city simultaneously carefree and strict, severe and roistering, was totally devoted to horsemanship. Masters and students at the cavalry school reigned over an equestrian city that lived for them. The French defeat of 1870–71, the arrival of the Prussians in Paris, the abdication of Napoleon III, the burning of the Tuileries—all this had occurred less than thirteen years before the birth of Gabrielle Chanel in 1883. The Empire was only yesterday, but the fashions of that era had already disappeared from the street. Among the cavalrymen, uniforms were now more severe, with a low képi replacing the tall shako as headgear. Still, there remained the frogs and loops, the passementerie braids, and on jackets (oh, Chanel!) nine gold buttons, the privilege of the military.

△ Saumur at the end of the 19th century. The horsemen of the Cadre Noir report to the manège ("riding academy"), their gold-banded whips held like scepters. Along the way, ladies are honored with devouring glances. On a balmy evening in Saumur the second lieutenants enjoy their street encounters with the so-called *cocottes avec équipage*. The women called "little allies" were not ruinous mistresses. A dinner here, a hat there—this was about all the young bucks of Saumur had to offer, leaving the street girls to live and die in poverty.

August in Saumur

This was the month of the Carrousel, the event of the year, the festival of festivals. That day the entire school could be found on the Chardonnet, the field where everything

happened—quadrilles, reviews, the presentation of troops, riding instructions.

On August 19, 1883, the female companion of a small-wares peddler hurried across the merry town, a lone figure directing her steps toward the hospital. There Jeanne Devolle gave birth to Gabrielle.

Stretching over the severe portico that once protected the entrance to a leper hospital of the Order of Saint-Jean are the words "Hospice Général." To give birth in the hospice was considered an indication of extreme poverty by middle-class ladies.

The birth of Gabrielle Chanel

On August 20, 1883, Gabrielle was taken to the town hall by three employees of the hospital. They registered her as the child of Albert Chanel, merchant, and a shop girl named Devolle, domiciled "with her husband." The latter was absent. No one knew the exact spelling of Chanel, so the mayor improvised, adding an "s" to the

◁ The pursuit of women, a sport like any other.

△ The Hospice General in Saumur where Jeanne Devolle gave birth to Gabrielle.

No 212.

Chasnel
Gabrielle

L'an mil huit cent quatre-vingt-trois, le *Vingt Aout* à quatre heures du soir par devant nous *François Poitou, adjoint délégué du* Maire de la ville de Saumur, département de Maine-et-Loire, remplissant les fonctions d'officier public de l'État-Civil a comparu à la Mairie Mme *Joséphine Pélerin, Célibataire, âgée de Soixante deux ans, employée à l'hospice de cette ville et y demeurant* Lequel nous a présenté un enfant du sexe *Féminin* né au domicile de l'hospice en cette ville le jour d'hier à quatre heures du soir issu de *Henri Chasnel, Marchand âgé de Vingt huit ans, né à Nimes (Gard) domicilié à Saumur rue St Jean 29 et Eugénie Jeanne Dévolles, Marchande, âgée de Vingt ans, née à Courpierres département du Puy de Dôme, domiciliée avec son mari.* auquel enfant il a été donné le prénom de *Gabrielle* Lesquelles présentation et déclaration ont été faites en présence de M *Jacques Sureau* âgé de *Soixante douze ans* profession de *Employé à l'hospice*, domicilié à *Saumur* et de M *Ambroise Pordestail* âgé de *Soixante deux ans* profession de *Employé à l'hospice* domicilié à *Saumur* Et n'ont pas signé le présent acte avec nous, lecture faite ayant dit ne savoir

infant's paternal name. The three members of the hospital staff were all illiterate. Consequently, an age-old formula had to be used: "Having said they did not know how to read, they did not sign the present document, which was read aloud." The mayor then signed what otherwise would have been a virtually anonymous paper.

△ The birth certificate of Gabrielle Chanel, 1883.

At the races, women all but effaced by ornament

The inauguration in 1877 of the racetrack at Verrie was a very important date in the history of the Saumur cavalry school.

The races at Verrie were an event, but one that produced more sport than elegance. The dreaded dust caused women to envelop their faces in veils as thick as curtains, which hung from hats that looked like huge eggs stuffed with flowers and ribbons.

As shown in late-19th-century photographs, the entire school at Saumur—lieutenants, second lieutenants, and horsemen, black jackets and blue jackets (never pale enough for the men of the light-horse!), training horses, race horses and cavalry horses—whipped itself into a murderous frenzy while participating in notoriously difficult trials. It took a total of seventy-seven falls to make

a cavalryman. Some Sundays at Verrie more spills were registered than starts. No one at the finish! Crazy officers. But what charm! What elegance! With their foulard caps, slender waists (corseted, some said), perfectly fitted jackets, and collars that could never be too high, men indisputably had the advantage in that fin-de-siècle era. Meanwhile women—with their overload of ornament—looked like haystacks.

△ At the races, men looked almost modern with their form-fitting attire compared to the women whose overly adorned dresses and enormous hats were very much of the 19th century.

Life in the public markets

In 1884 Gabrielle's mother was offered what she had long despaired of: marriage to Albert Chanel, with whom she had been living for three years. In the margin of the marriage certificate appear the names of two children—Julia and Gabrielle—whom Albert recognized as his. Together—he very much the cock of the village walk, she sweet and submissive—they brought up their daughters in the public markets. Very few French cities provided covered markets in those days. Fairs, religious festivals, peasant gatherings involving entire families—all took place out-of-doors, with merchants and merchandise alike exposed to every kind of weather. It was in this humble world that Gabrielle spent her childhood. The greatest problem for itinerant merchants was to find a city to work from. For two years Albert made Issoire the point of departure for his peregrinations. From the small-wares peddler that he was, Albert Chanel evolved into a sort of traveling salesman specializing in work clothes and undergarments.

△ Note the marked contrast between the rich attire of the woman wearing a hat and the peasant dress of the *marchande*.

△ By the end of the 19th century, small country markets like this one were threatened by the lure of the city—the metropolis that consumed, perverted, and depopulated rural France.

◁ All the wretchedness of the late 19th century is expressed in the faces and forms of these women seated on a curbstone, offering their pitiful wares.

I. Coco, a kept woman

The abbey for orphan girls

Orphanage. If there is a word that never crossed the lips of Gabrielle Chanel, it was this one. She worked relentlessly to eradicate all traces of the unhappy fate that had been hers. When her mother died in 1895 Gabrielle was twelve years old. Following a move from Brive to Aubazine, Albert Chanel abandoned his daughters to the region's largest orphanage.

△ Bernard Boutet de Monvel, *The Orphans* or *The Pensionnat de Nemours*, 1909. Musée des Beaux-Arts, Pau.

▽ The vast halls, vaulted corridors, and echoing stairways of this monastic building once swarmed with black-clad orphans, whose sad existence Gabrielle and her sisters shared for six years.

Moulins, a city of Masses and processions

In 1900 young Gabrielle had to make a difficult choice. The Aubazine nuns kept no orphans beyond age eighteen, except those wishing to enter the novitiate. Gabrielle, with little interest in the religious life, found herself taken in by an institution in Moulins administered by a congregation of canonesses. There the occasions to go out were few, and the reason for them always had to be pious.

△ High Masses out-of-doors and slow processions unfolded in Moulins with more ceremony, it seemed, than anywhere else in France.

◁ The kiosk where the local band, La Lyre Moulinoise, could be heard. This, one said, was no place for convent girls, but Gabrielle longed to attend the concerts.

▽ Dressed alike, even to their straw hats, and flanked by priests in immaculate surplices, the handsome boys of Moulins were the city's principal Sunday attraction.

Worlds apart: demoiselles and charity cases

In addition to paying students, the boarding school that took in Gabrielle Chanel and her sisters admitted free of charge, as did many such institutions of the time, a certain number of young women without means. On one side of the school were the young ladies who obviously enjoyed material advantages and, on the other, the poor girls. It was in the latter category that the canonesses enrolled Gabrielle Chanel. Almost nineteen upon arrival, she remained two years, treated always like an orphan on charity. Not once did her father give any sign of life.

◁ The girls of the free school also wore *pèlerines*, but these were made of rough wool and knitted in the convent's workroom. The second-hand ankle boots were, like everything else, provided by the congregation.

△ Young women of a private boarding school at Moulins in 1895, all dressed in garnet-colored cashmere furnished by their families. The double wardrobe (for winter and summer) was both large and fine, consisting of "cap, straw boater, two dresses, two *pèlerines,* two cloaks, and two pairs of shoes at least."

△ During fairs, dog shearers served as coiffeurs. This made it possible to sell the tresses of penniless girls for a good price to ladies desiring additional hair, as well as to institutions teaching young women the art of embroidering with hair.

Chanel, shop girl

A peasant insistence upon making a clear separation between work clothes and Sunday dress—one functional, the other for show—and the conviction of people bound to the soil that only that which cannot be worn out should be used—all this Gabrielle Chanel had in her blood. When she was twenty, the canonesses placed her as a clerk in a thriving hosiery shop in Moulins run by some extremely decent folk. Indeed, it represented the height of elegance for the world about.

Those gentlemen of the 10th Chasseurs

Moulins could boast an important garrison. It billeted several regiments, but only one unit—and only from 1889 to 1913—really counted: the 10th Chasseurs, an aristocratic regiment and the ultra-smart club for sons of old families. The apprentice of the Rue de l'Horloge quickly became the toast of the young lieutenants. With Gabrielle's permission, these gallants made themselves her true discoverers. But the gentleman she came to prefer, the one who first loved her, was a young infantry officer whose family belonged to the Moulins district: Étienne Balsan, scion of the haute bourgeoisie and beneficiary of a considerable private income.

△ Gabrielle Chanel in 1903, when she was a shop girl in Moulins. With her, an officer of the 10th Chasseurs and one of her many admirers.

▷△ Moulins's Villars quarter billet of the Chasseurs, constructed during the reign of Louis-Philippe (1830–48).

▷▽ Étienne Balsan during his tour of duty with the 90th Infantry Regiment.

They called her Coco

Debuts at La Rotonde

It was at La Rotonde in Moulins that Gabrielle made her stage debut. The pavilion had been built around 1860 as a reading room, but, scarcely three years later, as the café-concert rage spread throughout France, it became the setting for the region's best-known *concert à quête*. The very term indicates that the young women employed there received payment mainly by passing the hat. It also served as a euphemism for *beuglant*—slang ("bellowing") meaning "concert hall" and also "low class"—which would hardly have appealed to an audience of officers. With admission free, spectators paid only for drinks.

◁ An 1885 announcement of the program of entertainment scheduled at La Rotonde in Moulins.

△ The program for *Ko Ko Ri Ko*, a successful review produced by P.L. Flers in 1897 at La Scala, a chic café-concert in Paris.

△ At La Rotonde, in 1904, one of the *poseuses* ("amateur artists" or "models") prepares to pass the hat between the tables, a ritual that had long been given up in Paris *caf'-concs*. Drawing by Ibels for *Les Demi-Cabots* (*The Semi-Actors*), which appeared in 1906.

◁ Singing "The Cavalrymen of Reichshoffen" was obligatory in concert halls catering to the military. Coiffed in a képi, an artiste led the songs most favored by the uniformed patriots.

At Moulins in 1905 there still appeared on stage those concert-hall performers known as *poseuses* ("models")—actually supers who ranged themselves in a semicircle behind the stars and sat there like well-behaved guests at a salon. Their role was to give the establishment an air of gentility and to fill in between numbers. Whenever the stage emptied, one *poseuse* at a time would come forward and perform her own little piece, usually in a manner more dead than alive. This was how Chanel made her debut at La Rotonde, with a repertoire consisting of two songs: "Ko Ko Ri Ko" and "Qui qu'a vu Coco." The audience then began calling her by the word that appeared in the refrain of both songs. Soon she became *la petite Coco* to all her fans at the garrison.

△ H. G. Ibels, drawing, published in 1906. Narrow stage, upright piano, and, behind the star, a circle of ladies *en peaux* ("in evening dress")—this was the *café-concert* formula. Engaged by the month, dismissed after two weeks, bombarded with cherry pits—such was the unenviable lot of a music-hall beginner.

◁ The poster for *Ko Ko Ri Ko*. The title song from this review and "Qui qu'a vu Coco" constituted the entire repertoire of Coco Chanel at the time of her arrival in the theatres at Vichy in 1906.

The nobodies of Vichy

Among other things to know about the Chanel family: Gabrielle's grandfather, when an old man, sired a daughter who was the same age as his granddaughter. This made the beautiful Adrienne the aunt of Gabrielle, even though she was often taken as the latter's sister. From the age of seventeen, the two young women were inseparable, sharing the life of charity pupils at a convent, the life of shop girls, and even the stage at La Rotonde, where Adrienne, perceived as having no vocal talent whatever, took charge of passing the plate. Thus, Adrienne followed when Gabrielle, who had great ambitions and dreamed of one day becoming the equal of Yvette Guilbert, left the Moulins café-concert for the "season" at Vichy, there to try her luck among the many music halls in what was France's most cosmopolitan watering place.

There is no doubt that Gabrielle Chanel tried more than one line of work in Vichy. Concert-hall engagements could not be picked up there as easily as in Moulins. But Gabrielle did take hope that she might

△ Like the young women in this 1902 photograph, Gabrielle worked for a while as a mineral-water dispenser (*donneuse d'eau*) in the pump room of the Grand Grill.

▷ Gabrielle (left) and Adrienne (right) Chanel at Vichy in 1906, wearing dresses and hats made entirely by themselves. This constitutes the earliest known document in which the Chanel style can be sensed.

eventually become a *gommeuse* ("envelope licker," slang for a promising beginner, but in this instance on the music-hall stage), if only she could develop her voice. The problem was to find the money, since singing and dancing lessons could not be had free. Gabrielle therefore found herself working as a mineral-water dispenser (*donneuse d'eau*) in the pump room of the Grand Grill. She donned a white uniform and, from the bottom of a strange pit surrounded by grillework, spent some time filling glasses and handing them to those in Vichy for the cure.

△ The *gommeuse* typically wore a spangled dress with a bodice that lent fullness to the bust. After hugging the hips, the skirt flared slightly to midcalf. A *gommeuse* had to be *décolletée* and show her legs. The somewhat perverse seductiveness of this costume—the charm of a style neither long nor short—would haunt and inspire Coco Chanel for the rest of her life.

In Belle Époque Vichy it was believed that music, light or classical, possessed curative powers at least equal to those of the mineral waters. Thus, the thermal season brought a veritable explosion of concerts. In the morning, a performance in the bandstand situated next to the spring known as La Source de l'Hôpital; in the afternoon, another one at the sidewalk cafés; and in the evening, four variety theatres offering the best of France's most acclaimed *fantaisistes*.

△ The façade of the Élysée Palace, one of Vichy's café-concerts at the beginning of the century.

The golden age of operetta

The sojourn that Gabrielle Chanel made at Vichy in 1906 yielded none of the opportunities that she had dreamed of. At auditions, which she undertook with the highest hope, impresarios found her full of undeniable grace, but regretted that such a delightful beginner lacked a voice. None of the great café-concerts could use her neither the Eden Theatre nor the Alcazar—for the shows in Vichy offered nothing but the best. Moreover, one no longer dared appear there as a *poseuse*, since a recent decree had banned the *poseuse* system as humiliating to the young women and inconsistent with the taste of a public now grown more sophisticated. Thus, Gabrielle took consolation in indulging her passion for the theatre, and in Vichy she discovered a type of show then becoming the rage: operetta.

Operettas are light, pleasant, and entertaining, the predecessor of the Broadway muscial and an offshoot of

△▷ Cover and inside page of a program for the Scala Theatre during the initial production of *Ko Ko Ri Ko*, the review in which Polaire scintillated and whose theme song became the main vehicle for Coco Chanel at a time when her ambition was to become an operetta star.

the opéra-comique. The operetta originated in Vienna and quickly arrived in Paris, then under the giddy reign of the Second Empire. The new form of lyric theatre had spoken dialogue as well as arias set to light music that was catchy and easy to listen to. In contrast to the great tragedies of classical opera, operettas were usually frivolous, often downright sexy, and always blessed with happy endings. The point was to amuse a nouveau-riche public rapidly evolving into the Belle Époque.

The great hits had hardly been put on in Paris before they went to Vichy in productions fully equal to those of the capital. Stars and richly produced programs were all to be found in Vichy. The haunt of divas and divettes, the spa in season became an important center of music, attracting a titled audience of Russian aristocrats, Oriental princes, crowned heads, and virtually everyone of importance in the world of business and politics.

overleaf: Details of the inside page of the Scala Theatre program.

A *gommeuse* without a future

Adieu Paris! Since she had abandoned all hope of a stage career in the capital and since success otherwise remained elusive, Gabrielle Chanel had no choice but to accept the provinces and to live there as best she could. Here, therefore, is Gabrielle at a crucial moment in her life. It is Sunday at the races in Vichy, with Chanel wearing a dress and hat made by herself. Does one see only Chanel? If so, it is because a complete naturalness sets her apart from the other women. Also because her hat would seem smart even today. Clearly, she is ready to bury those costly bird coffins with which her neighbors have dressed their heads. Moreover, Chanel alone wears her hair over the brow. In 1907 she inaugurated the bangs that would become the hair style of every emancipated woman of the 1920s. But note also the collar—the eternal little white collar, unrecognized but already a Chanel trademark. Nearby is Adrienne, a less daring figure, who conforms to the fashion of the day.

▷ Not in the box of the landed gentry, but among the bourgeois of the region, Adrienne, on the left, in jabot and high style; Gabrielle, on the right (and in the detail above), simply clothed with a turned-down collar; and, between them, a new, opulent figure, her stature and her plume towering over all else. This is Maud, a friend of the Chanel girls who would play the complex role of counselor, duenna, and chaperone to Adrienne.

Adrienne and her chaperone

When the season at Vichy came to an end and the café-concerts had their annual closing without even the smallest contract having been offered, the young Gabrielle no longer had any illusions: a stage career would not be hers. Thus, she gave up the idea of the theatre and returned to Moulins and to her old life—evenings at La Rotonde and flirtation with cavalry officers.

Still, a great change had come about. Adrienne, Gabrielle's young aunt and childhood friend, no longer resided in Moulins. She remained in the district, but living at Souvigny, in the home of an intimate friend, Maud Mazuel, who became her impresario. Without taking Adrienne away from her original "cavalier" entourage, Maud had introduced her to some of the château nobility, older than the lieutenants of the 10th Chasseurs, but endowed with greater means and more freedom.

△ Adrienne (left) and Maud (right) in 1909 at a photographer's studio.

The indispensable duenna

Maud, although not beautiful, had spirit, self-assurance, and, when necessary, the air of a woman of rank, whose identification with the past was evident in her Louis XV jabots, her hats *à la mousquetaire*, and the cut of her suits, with their long slanting coattails reminiscent of the Directoire period.

Maud divided herself between two contradictory vocations: the life of any party and chaperone. She was equally skilled in both roles. A *demoiselle*, Maud had a great appetite for society and a keen desire to succeed in it. Born to a different milieu, she would have maintained a salon, but her obscure origins rendered this impossible. Thus, she made do by arranging encounters and perhaps in facilitating liaisons.

Adrienne used Maud as a means to ends that would otherwise have been unimaginable. In the person of her

△ Fashion was a torture. Here is an *élégante* marching, doing her breathing exercises, and about to leave for the country. As Paul Morand wrote, "Underneath a corset, a lady's chest was compressed by several layers of lacing."

Mlle Cécile Sorel
Sociétaire de la Comédie-Française
dans le "Demi-Monde"

hostess, duly whaleboned, corseted, sheathed, and hat-ted, Adrienne found the indispensable duenna, the ideal chaperone without whom a young woman such as she—child of the people, devoid of means or family, yet ambi-tious, however foolishly, to enter society—would not have had the slightest chance of success. Maud would be the solid guarantee of Adrienne's respectability.

One lady and three admirers

Through Maud, the country squires had met provincial divorcées and a few well-known, much-admired *irreg-ulières* ("irregular" women because unmarried to the men they lived with), but none of these could match the love-liness, the figure, the proud bearing, the royal manner of Adrienne. Thus, not one suitor attached himself to her, but three!

It was the Comte de Beynac, an aggressively musta-chioed aristocrat with solid connections among the old

◁ Adrienne flanked on her right by the Marquis de Jumilhac and on her left by the man who would become the sole love of her life.

△ Coincidence? In Vichy, Adrienne adopted the ample ostrich plumes and large felt form worn by Cécile Sorel in 1911 when, for the Comédie-Française, she played the lead in a revival of *Le Demi-Monde*, the comedy of 1850 by Alexandre Dumas *fils*. Judged "immoral and shocking" when first produced, the play was now accepted without difficulty, thanks to the art of la Sorel in the role of a coquette—beautiful, frivolous, delightful, and a bit fierce.

landed gentry, who discovered Adrienne and who no doubt was her official "protector." More than three-quarters ruined, he nonetheless had in the person of a great friend—the Marquis de Jumilhac—a sort of Maecenas who always seemed ready to encourage his pranks. Both Beynac and Jumilhac served as mentors to a young man, the son of a local chatelain, who, being clever enough to learn from his friends' savoir-faire, had quickly become a "clubman" of indisputable charm.

Here, therefore, was a trio of admirers who vied for the heart of Adrienne. By common consent, they decided to propose a trip to Egypt, where the object of their attentions could freely choose the one among them she would most prefer.

△ To everyone in Vichy who saw her attending the races in a fine carriage, ravishingly turned out, and always in the company of a young man of old family, Adrienne appeared to be a woman of infinite daring. The plumed hat was still de rigueur, a "must" particularly since it was less a fashion than a social privilege.

**The 1900s style
throws off its last sparks**

The Gilded Age with its fancy dresses and
overly decorated hats was fading away
while an unknown young woman,
Gabrielle Chanel, was evolving from her
state as a kept woman to that of a dressmaker. Her future was very promising.
Veber, *Chez la modiste*, lithograph, 1907.

The duel between horse and motor

Taken from Great Britain, the taste for the out-of-doors spread throughout the Parisian *gratin* ("upper crust"), a class of people Anglophobic in politics and Anglophilic in style. With the first good days of spring, the lovers of fresh air mounted the mail coaches for picnics in the country. But the women went in the same finery they wore in town.

Long skirts, fragile hats, narrow shoes with high heels—all that could impede walking and make women seem

△ At the same time that the garage was assuming more and more of the space once reserved for stables in the outbuildings of private residences, the first motorbuses appeared in the streets of Paris.

helpless—filled their husbands with self-importance. With wives unable to put one foot in front of the other unaided, the open-air craze could not but enhance the authority of men.

At the same time that the garage was assuming more and more of the space once reserved for stables in the outbuildings of private residences, the first motorbuses appeared in the streets of Paris. The scene opposite is the Avenue du Bois in December 1905, during the fifth Salon d'Auto, with the very latest motor vehicles driven by their owners. For the sake of trying out the newest thing, women perched on the front seat next to the driver and allowed themselves to be ogled.

Masters and mistresses

Chanel was twenty-five when she agreed to live with Étienne Balsan, the man who would lead her out of provincial backwaters and into château life. How could she have imagined that the new situation would offer so little change from all she had wanted to escape in Moulins? On the delicate face under the immense black hat can be detected the traces of a bitter disappointment.

Suzanne or the demimonde

The lovely Suzanne Orlandi was typical of the young friends about whom Gabrielle, once she had become the famous Mademoiselle Chanel, would never speak. Perhaps it was because their fate had too many points in common with her own. Suzanne proved more than discreet concerning the misery of their youth, their struggles, their disappointments, the affronts they suffered—and discreet on the subject of their love affairs. Not a word would she utter. But this made

△ In 1907, at Robinson, an outing on donkey-back for horsemen (breeders, trainers) and their *petites amies*. From left to right: Maurice Caillaux and Mlle Fourchemer, Suzanne Orlandi and Baron Foy, Chanel and Balsan. The pluckiness of Chanel's little bow tie offers a kind of male simplicity in contrast to the boned collars and Henri II ruffs that still encumber the other *amazones*.

her no less an irrefutable witness, which, in the mind of Gabrielle, constituted sufficient reason never to invoke the name of Suzanne Orlandi. Both belonged to that social category situated between *le monde*, the world qualifying as "society," and the other realm known as *le monde de la galanterie.* In other words, they occupied the *demimonde*—the "half-world"—a term that came into general usage with the successful play of that title by Alexandre Dumas *fils*. And the author had taken pains to give the definition that appeared in the dictionary as soon as the word had been created: "The demimonde? A comedown for women who have left a high place, a summit for those who have left a low one." Gabrielle and Suzanne started from the bottom.

And a woman of this half-world could expect nothing but a half-reality. It was imperative that she live unac-

△ Near Negrine during a voyage to Algeria, Suzanne Orlandi with Baron Foy.

knowledged, because, in the eyes of families, she was a greater threat than the celebrated courtesans who haunted Maxim's. These, at least, played a very straightforward game; they were paid, and for the services rendered no one expected them to be sweet, simple, and good. But a young, unknown woman? A man could become so infatuated that he might be persuaded to offer the respectability of marriage. Horrors! Marry a nobody without fortune, family, or even a couturier—a parvenue who dressed herself and made her own hats!

Coco, however, enjoyed one bit of good luck: she did not have to suffer the opprobrium of Balsan's relatives. Having been orphaned, he could live with Coco as he wished. Meanwhile, Suzanne, as well as Adrienne, would

suffer endless humiliation. The families of the men they loved refused to receive them. Any trip they made in the company of their lovers had to be to a country where *le monde* never went, owing to its distance, danger, or discomfort. Thus, both Suzanne and Adrienne found themselves traveling in the only direction then possible under the circumstances—to Africa. There, however, one could be at peace, for neither the habitués of the Deauville boardwalks nor the great huntsmen of Chantilly would have ventured so far.

△ Born of a richly maintained opera singer and a father whose identity could never be disclosed, Suzanne loved to adopt theatrical attitudes and disguises. Here she is in a burnoose posing in the Aurès Mountains of Algeria.

Émilienne, courtesan and poet

Who was Émilienne d'Alençon? For some, a brave girl; for others, a monster. In reality, she was the child of concierges in the Rue des Martyrs who earned a special place among the great hetaeras reigning at the turn of the century. *La petite Coco*, a young unknown barely out of her native province, was presented to Émilienne in the home of Étienne Balsan.

Balsan, at the time of his encounter with Gabrielle Chanel, had the look of a young man of means making his mark in all the fashionable places. And he took a not-inconsiderable pride in the mastery with which he had succeeded in casting off Émilienne after a whirlwind affair. Of all the courtesans of the era, this one was reputed to have the most voracious appetites. Did she not, without batting an eye, ruin the young Duc d'Uzès? Moreover, there was no one in Paris who did not know for a fact that eight members of the Jockey Club had pooled their resources and formed a kind of corporation whose sole purpose was to secure the lady's favors on a regular basis. But all that had finished by 1907, and thereafter the famous *femme*

△ Émilienne d'Alençon at the peak of her glory. One soon forgot that she was the daughter of concierges and had been christened simply Émilienne André.

fatale no longer had any interest in seizing the assets of ducal heirs or the family jewels of an old, bearded sovereign. Having made her fortune, Émilienne only thought about her literary ambitions. She saw herself as a poet, and wore winged collars. Actually, while still a great favorite of the scandal sheets, she had become a bit passée in the demimonde. At thirty-three, Émilienne found one of her latest passions in Alec Carter, the jockey with three hundred victories to his credit and the idol of the whole turf crowd.

△ Émilienne d'Alençon in a straw boater and wing collar.

▷▷▷ The little boater (detail left), born in 1910 on a windy day, would always be the type of hat Chanel preferred, and she made it the height of fashion for half a century.

▽ Women and fashions that Coco avoided.

White collar, necktie, and straw boater

Gabrielle Chanel was twenty-six when, standing on a bench at a racecourse in the South of France, with binoculars hung about her neck bandolier-style, she watched the training of one of the Balsan horses. From head to toe, everything about her is simple, fashionless, and sporty. She had made herself a trim little hat suited to the open-air circumstances and secured it with a huge pin against the blustery winds of the mistral. If she has a jaunty look, it is due to the bulky, well-tailored coat borrowed from Baron Foy and the silk tie from Balsan, both of whom were astounded by her mania for stealing their clothes. But little could Coco imagine that her improvised ensemble constituted the first draft of a style that, twenty years later when she had become a renowned couturière, would have women all over the world wearing white collars, neckties, and boaters.

Émilienne d'Alençon, who added a big ribbon to her straw hat.

Cécile Sorel coiffed in a plumed boater.

Defying fashion

Going from track to track—this was how one lived with Étienne Balsan. But Coco had to keep to the grass, since she could not risk encountering some lady or other who might be offended by the sight of the woman Balsan was living with. In her obsessive fear of being taken for a cocotte, Gabrielle observed the proprieties to excess. At all cost, she had to set herself apart from everyone else in her position. Thus, she could have been taken for the most straightforward of young women, coiffed in one of the straw boaters she made for herself and that enchanted her friends. One of Coco's hats caught the fancy of Émilienne d'Alençon, after which the great courtesan never wore anything but boaters, although overloading them with a thousand personal embellishments. From now on there was no denying the influence of Gabrielle Chanel, which grew until it reached beyond her circle of friends.

A certain idea of the body

By 1909 Gabrielle Chanel had developed into this beauty with the heavy dark hair, the small turned-up nose, the marvelous profile—a young woman who was just now beginning to make a name for herself. She sits straight (opposite), as she would all her life, perched on every chair as if on horseback, or as if by wearing an easier, more fluid dress than that of her contemporaries (in a dress here that she created), she had already become convinced that being fit counted for more than a corset. This was radical, her idea of the body. If Chanel did not yet know quite what she wanted, her infallible instinct told her precisely what she did not want. All the fashions of the day, with their complicated graces, struck her as ridiculous. She was four years ahead of her time.

◁ An *élégante* at the Longchamp races, 1913.

△ Madame Mona Deiza, a star of the Vaudeville theatre, 1912.

▷ Chanel in 1909, with neither pearls nor lace. Under her dress she wears a *modestie* trimmed with ribbon, as simple and attractive as a convent pinafore.

The fun-loving Balsan set

Among other advantages, Balsan's hospitality was open to everything but snobbery. Étienne had banished the whole lot of virtuous wives and formidable dowagers, and allowed everyone to live sheltered from what Proust called "the pitiless glare of lorgnettes." Whom did he gather about him? Mainly stars of sport and theatre, all free spirits who did not count "virtue" among the foremost of their qualities, but who otherwise were more attractive than the milieu in which Gabrielle had begun her independent social life in Moulins and Vichy.

Among the habitués of Balsan's household could be found a second and brilliant Gabrielle in the person of a young actress then just making her mark: Gabrielle Dorziat. Another actress was Jeanne Lery, whom the Grand Duke Boris had abandoned after a long liaison. As for the men, they formed a band of horse lovers who fully appreciated a household in which it was possible to enjoy the rare pleasure of living freely with their mistresses. All of Balsan's friends—male and female—participated in their host's favorite pastimes, which consisted of casually

△ One evening the Balsan gang improvised *Une Noce campagnarde* (*A Country Wedding*), a production costumed by Gabrielle. From left to right: Gabrielle as best man, Balsan, Lery as the bride and Henraux as the groom, and Arthur Capel as mother-in-law. Seated: Comte de Laborde playing the newlyweds' baby and Gabrielle Dorziat the maid of honor. On Capel's head, the ribbon "cabbage" that Gabrielle had worn as the *chaisière* (chair attendant in the park). At Balsan's a good time could be had at little expense to anyone. In the photographs, however, no smile ever crosses the face of Gabrielle Chanel.

▷ Here one morning, a bathrobed Gabrielle Chanel reads her newspaper after having appeared at breakfast disguised as a *chaisière*.

organized evenings and grand entrances in disguise, with
the events recorded by camera. It was an enchanting and
carefree world that was soon to come to an end.

Laughter replaces luxury

The change is evident, for even in their amusements the Balsan crowd challenged the Belle Époque. With them a whole era of Parisian life came to an end, an era that had turned frivolity into a costly obligation. Even though Balsan had certainly slept with Émilienne d'Alençon, she was already, in the eyes of his friends, a person from another age.

Here Chanel impersonates a timid adolescent boy, escorting Dorziat's village girl whose socks are too short

△ The two Gabrielles, Dorziat and Chanel, as maid and man of honor at a village wedding, dressed in what Chanel had been able to purchase at the most popular of the period's great stores: La Samaritaine. Had a woman of fashion dared to set foot there, the newspapers would have sent photographers.

and whose skirt is too long. For Gabrielle, the jacket worn over a white vest, the shirt with its Peter Pan collar and its cuffs extended beyond the coat sleeves, the softly knotted bow tie, the white "Breton" hat with its turned-up brim, the snowy gloves slipped into the breast pocket, no doubt for the want of a handkerchief—all this, bought in the boys' department of a department store, constitutes a sketch for what would become the Chanel style. While playing a game, Gabrielle had discovered the fundamental principle of her art: elements of male attire adapted for feminine use.

◁ At an Opéra ball, Émilienne dressed as Columbine, coiffed in a cocked hat of fresh flowers and adorned with her famous three-strand necklace of pearls.

△ At the height of the Belle Époque it was considered extremely daring for a woman to appear on the stage in tight culottes. When Émilienne d'Alençon took the risk, she was the first, doing so in 1889 at the Cirque d'Été. Here she is in 1910, a rather buxom Harlequin with massive thighs and a quilted doublet ornamented with bells.

Sarah Bernhardt at her zenith

The one called "*l'Unique*" or, more familiarly, Madame Sarah, was, around 1907, at the time of a poetry recital, the first tragedienne that Chanel had ever seen. Bernhardt's voice was compared to a golden bell, and Oscar Wilde called her "the divine Sarah." She was the most famous actress of her time, had her own theatre that bore her name in Paris, and toured throughout the entire world.

Chanel loved to describe the event to which Adrienne Chanel had invited her in Paris. But is it credible that Gabrielle never shared the admiration with which her contemporaries overwhelmed the great actress? "She was laughable!" Chanel insisted, "An old clown . . . . And then that pinched voice . . . nasal! I could not bear it. Whereas Duse! Now, there was a woman, not a Byzantine Punch and Judy show!" Then followed an imitation of her *bête noire* in *L'Aiglon*, with legs spread wide like a man in a parody of the great Bernhardt playing Napoleon's ill-fated son.

△◁ Sarah Bernhardt in Victorien Sardou's *Théodora*, 1884.

△ In 1923, at seventy-nine years of age, Sarah Bernhardt agreed to appear in a movie. Here she is in *La Voyante*, filmed in her home at 56, boulevard Pereire, which for the occasion was transformed into a studio. She died three days after the end of shooting, which had been completed in two weeks of daily work. Mary Marquet, who with Harry Baur gave the old actress her cues, recalled in her memoirs "the poor figure all but collapsed in upon herself. . . ." Fifty thousand Parisians filed by the bier. Among them was Gabrielle Chanel.

◁ Georges Clairin, *Sarah Bernhardt*, 1876. Musée du Petit-Palais, Paris.

◁ The gatehouse at Royallieu.

◁◁ At Royallieu, reading the newspapers every morning on the terrace was an immutable rite. All the dailies of the period devoted an entire page to news of the turf and several columns to a minute description of the latest outfits worn by the cocottes, the true queens of *le Tout-Paris*. From left to right: Chanel in a suit, *claudine* or "school girl" collar, and a white *lavallière*; Lucien Henraux in leggings reading *Le Journal*; and Gabrielle Dorziat wearing a riding habit while immersed in *L'Excelsior*.

▽ The thick mass of Gabrielle's hair was gathered at the nape of her neck in a sumptuous chignon.

Château life

To receive an invitation to Royallieu, a woman had to be fun-loving, capable of wearing boots the whole time, and willing to gallop all day long from one end of the forest to the other. Gabrielle Chanel, having become the mistress of Étienne Balsan, found herself living intimately with a man who was the very incarnation of the sportsman type, oblivious to the world except that part of it where horses raced, seeing only a few close friends, ladies of the demi-monde, and jockeys.

The Château de Royallieu was at the center of a region where horses counted for more than anything else. Balsan took up residence there, for an article of faith held that a thoroughbred, in order to realize its promise, had to be trained in the Compiègne region and nowhere else. Here could be found entire dynasties of trainers who had come from England and established themselves in France. Chantilly and Maisons-Lafitte were now veritable English villages. Horses and horses alone—Balsan gave them the greatest part of his time and resources, and undoubtedly his stables ranked among the best in France. As for Gabrielle at Royallieu, her expectations were not excessive, but she insisted on having them all and immediately:

to sleep as long as she wished, to become the best horse-woman at Royallieu, and to think of nothing—in other words, to beat the Balsan crowd at their own game. She succeeded marvelously.

In the horse country

By reason of a natural shyness as much as for pleasure, Chanel spent the first months of her stay at Royallieu without leaving the estate. Actually, everything about the château overwhelmed her: the beauty of the park, the scale of the house and its stables, the luxury that surpassed all she had ever known.

The stables dethrone the paddock

"Chanel had only to appear in order to make the whole prewar mode fade away, causing Worth and Paquin to wither and die. She was a shepherdess. To her, the training course, boot leather, hay, horse dung, the forest interior, saddle soap—all smelled sweet." This is how Paul Morand, a friend and confidant, described Chanel's

△ Royallieu was once an abbey whose park had been planted with splendid trees. The abbey, although rebuilt in the 17th century by Benedictine nuns, had been founded by monks in 1303.

△▷ Gabrielle Chanel with Baron Foy.

▷▷ Gabrielle Chanel in 1912. By stripping her wardrobe of every embellishment, she hoped to escape the reputation she most dreaded: that of the kept woman. Still, Chanel became Balsan's *irrégulière* in the eyes of all who viewed her isolation as proof that she had something to hide.

▷ Gabrielle Dorziat in riding habit. The celebrated actress wears a headband of white piqué like those common among women in tennis. Created by Gabrielle, such a headpiece for galloping through the forest was deemed pure bad taste by society horsewomen who preferred *tricornes* or top hats.

attitude. Then he added that Gabrielle belonged to "that avant-garde of country girls in underskirts and flat shoes characterized by Marivaux; girls who go out, confront the dangers of the city, and triumph, doing so with the kind of solid appetite for vengeance that revolutions are made of." With Chanel began an elegance in reverse, which brought an end to parade clothes. She would not join the women who caracoled along the Avenue du Bois or those who strutted in the enclosures that were forbidden to her. The day was coming when simplicity would prevail in a world where women, as Chanel phrased it herself, had once been nothing but an excuse for embellishment, for laces, etc. According to Chanel, the stables would dethrone the paddock.

△ At the stables of Royallieu, equestrians in shirtsleeves. Gabrielle, still afraid to expose her face to the sun, wears what is nothing but a large felt hat-form, pulled down over the ears. With her are the elegant Léon de Laborde, at center, and Étienne Balsan.

▷ Boy Capel, Balsan's best friend, and Chanel on horseback. An outrage in the eyes of the fashionable world, Chanel wears jodhpurs, the model for which she obtained from a groom and had copied by a local tailor.

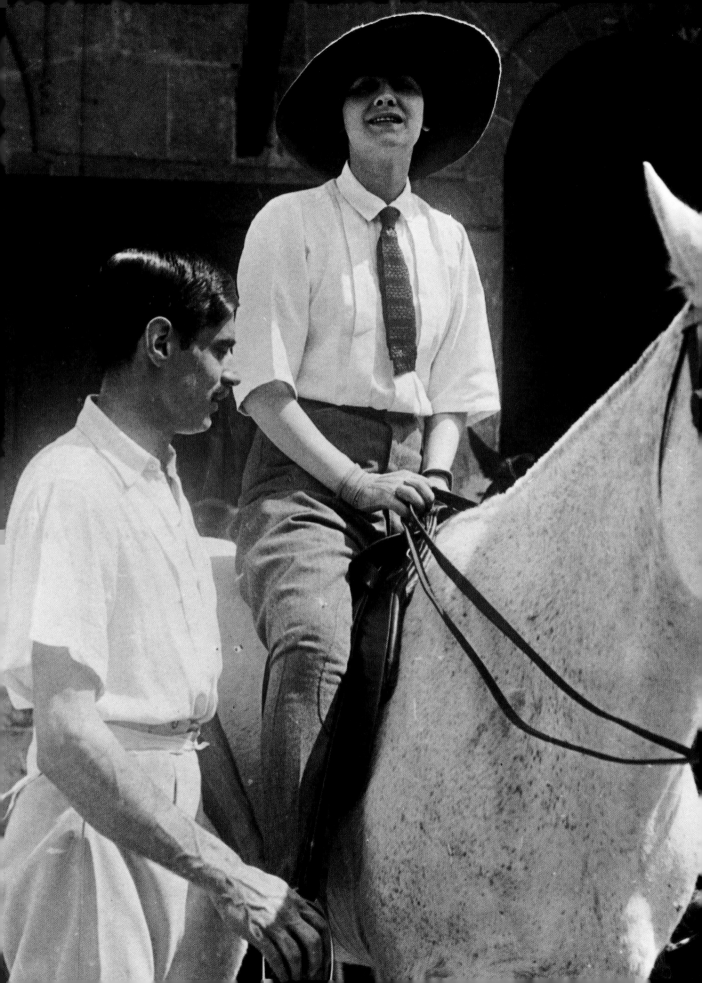

△ At the Deauville Grand Prix in 1907, women leaving the paddock. Kept women were excluded from the enclosure; only society ladies could make their glorious appearance there, dressed in white linen and Swiss muslin, embroidered and carefully worked—a nightmare for their maids.

△ Morning along the Avenue du Bois in 1912. The proud parade of corseted horsewomen, riders in top hats, beautiful mounts, the finest equipages, the most recent automobiles. It all made for a perfect elegance reigning over a splendid ennui.

A change of lifestyle

All of Balsan's friends noticed it. During the spring of 1912 an intimate friend of Étienne's, but a new habitué at Royallieu, appeared at the château with increasing frequency, all the while showing more and more interest in the charms of Gabrielle Chanel. The group had expanded to include an Englishman with thick black hair, a charmer whom every woman adored and who pursued the life of a self-made man. His name was Arthur Capel, known to his friends as "Boy." In Boy, Gabrielle Chanel found what she had vainly sought in Balsan—help and encouragement. Between Gabrielle and Étienne had arisen the first dissension concerning the eagerness she now felt to change her way of life. What did she want? To work. Her idleness weighed on Coco. She was bored. She wanted to go to Paris and make a career for herself as a *modiste*—a milliner. It was not that Étienne opposed the idea, but that he pretended to see the project as nothing more than a lark, whereas Gabrielle spoke in terms of a real métier. She did not wish merely to amuse herself concocting hats for friends, but rather to sell the creations and make a name for herself. Only Boy saw merit in the idea.

△ Scene of feigned jealousy in morning deshabille. Arthur Capel, in satin kimono, menacing Léon de Laborde, in short pajamas. In his arms, Gabrielle, wrapped in a bathrobe, her beautiful long hair falling about her shoulders.

Life with Boy

In high society and in Paris most of all, the French were Anglophobes in politics while sheer snobbery made them Anglophiles in their way of life. This helps explain the surprising popularity of Arthur Capel in Paris. What did anyone know about him? He had spent the greater part of his youth in English boarding schools: Beaumont, a Jesuit institution for the sons of Catholic gentlemen, and then Downside, run by the Benedictines and somewhat less uppercrust in social standing. But a great mystery surrounded his birth. Never did Boy mention his mother. Allegedly he was the natural son of a Frenchman who died shortly before Boy had finished his studies. This gave him something in common with Chanel: orphanhood. As for the identity of his father, the name most often proposed was Pereire. Boy Capel may have been the bastard son of the great banker and, moreover, part Jewish. There was no doubt, however, that in London Boy had been received in the most exclusive circles. Thus, because the English appreciated his rare abilities in polo and found it amusing and original that he took pleasure in working and earning money, Parisians resolved to do as much, to the point where no one bothered about the secrets of his birth. Personal attractiveness and his skill at cultivating the interests he owned in the coal fields of Newcastle simply added to the prestige enjoyed by Boy Capel.

△ Breakfast at Royallieu, the happy band of equestrians: Boy (from the back), Léon de Laborde (left), Gabrielle Dorziat, Étienne Balsan, Lucien Henraux, Gabrielle Chanel, and Jeanne Lery. The photos seen on these two pages were taken early in the summer of 1912.

overleaf: Coco Chanel, Étienne Balsan, and Boy Capel in the salon at Royallieu.

An irresistible man

To set Chanel up in Paris presented a number of problems, and Étienne Balsan hesitated. Buy her a business?
He laughed at the opinion of others—Boy's for
instance—as long as the little nobody from Vichy lived
discreetly. Maintaining and living with a mistress was a
situation that didn't need formalizing. But allow her to
work? What a scandal! Then, too, like so many former
cavalry officers, he liked spending money only so long as
it was for horses. In the end, Étienne thought to solve the
problem by offering Chanel, in lieu of a professional
space, the *garconnière* ("bachelor's chambers") he
owned on the ground floor at 160, boulevard
Malesherbes.

Foolish man! Boy lived nearby, and right away he began
making neighborly calls. Chanel, charming and still

△ Boy in Morocco. Marshal Lyautey,
who made Morocco a French
protectorate, had not been in Fez a
full year when Capel was already
investing, and also talking about
making Casablanca a great port for
the importation of English coal.

dressed like a boarding-school girl, simply drank in his every last word. Moreover, success did not wait long to embrace Coco's millinery efforts. Women were mad about Chanel hats. The beauteous friends of Balsan and Boy seemed to fall all over one another to buy the little orphan's boaters. Boy offered copious amounts of advice, while Balsan grew all the more annoyed. His best friend taking work seriously, and especially the work of Gabrielle!

Finally, the reason for Capel's *parti pris* became shockingly clear: Boy was in love with Coco. What was more, he admitted it. Balsan played the good prince and continued to let Gabrielle have the *garconnière,* although he knew that she was now living with Boy. Coco even returned to Royallieu with him, but only as a guest. She seemed to be a different woman.

△ Under a bowler hat, Chanel's ponytail was a shattering audacity. Even when dressed for riding, an elegant woman could not give up her "ratted," raised, and heavily supplemented coiffure, which no one described better than Marcel Proust. The well-cut riding habit worn by Chanel indicated, all by itself, that a change had occurred in her life.

Gabrielle Chanel stated upon a number of occasions that she had loved but once in her life and only once had known a man who seemed created for her: Arthur Capel. And it is almost certain that for once she spoke the truth.

Chanel loved everything about Capel. "More than handsome," she said, "he was magnificent." Coco admired everything about him; his eyes that looked at her with authority, his black hair, so deep a black that it seemed to make his face look encircled in jet. She even liked his foreign accent, also his feigned nonchalance. "He had a very strong, very individual personality, an ardent and concentrated nature." Never before could she have imagined life with a man who was at once athletic, enterprising, literate, and, despite his youth, already an important businessman. Gabrielle, of course, had known only young men more gifted in diminishing their fortunes than in adding to them.

Until then Chanel had lived happily enough, but always with the secret hope of breaking free of the mediocre role to which she had been limited, first by the self-centered and frivolous officers at Moulins and then, at Royallieu, by Étienne Balsan, who, while certainly a decent fellow with a sincere affection for her, was idle and too preoccupied with his horses and his equestrian success to take seriously the aspirations of his beautiful companion.

Finished were the band of crazy friends and the gallops through the forest. Soon to be finished also was Coco Chanel's work as a *modiste* in inadequate quarters whose address could not inspire confidence. At the beginning, of course, *la mode en garçonnière* seemed irresistibly amusing, for Gabrielle as much as for the carefree habitués of Royallieu.

In February 1910 Coco had been encamped there a year, lodged at the expense of Étienne on the Boulevard Malesherbes, where she made do in the cramped space of a ground-floor apartment. But despite the problems of such an arrangement, Chanel saw her clientele increase day by day: "The customers simply arrived, at first out of curiosity. One day I received a visit from a lady who frankly admitted: 'I've come . . . to see you.' I was a strange bird, a little lady with a boater on her head and her head on her shoulders."

▷ Arthur Capel in his ground-floor apartment on the Boulevard Malesherbes. With him Gabrielle Chanel discovered that one could be both a champion polo player and a lover of literature.

△ Of all Chanel's friends, Paul Morand was the one who had known Capel the best and unquestionably the one with whom she most enjoyed talking about this exceptional man. Morand himself had felt the fascination of Boy. And the two shared certain irresistible penchants—for fast living, luxury, record-breaking sports, horses, worldly quick conquest, and adventurous women. They also shared a great appetite for people and for life touched by a certain dandyism, which was nothing more than a façade masking their fear of seeming too serious. It should be no surprise that Boy became the subject of a Morand novel. "This Lewis who somewhat recalls Boy Capel" was the dedication the author wrote in the copy of *Lewis et Irène* (above) that Chanel kept in her library. A close reading reveals the character Lewis to have been drawn almost completely from Boy—"Beautiful quick brown eyes, a strong chin, and massively thick, black hair . . ." and a bit of Coco in Irène: "You are a businesswoman because you know how to survive." In addition, throughout the book, and barely altered, there are numerous aspects of Coco's life with Boy in Paris, from the time of their first encounter: "They saw no one. People annoyed Irène. . . ." The novel can, in large measure, be taken as a portrait of the Chanel–Capel liaison.

A generous lover

Gabrielle wanted to affirm herself and advance her business, to achieve success. And now an exceptional person showed interest in her. A new life was opening for her, a new life forever.

A question remained unanswered: To break or not? How could she forget what she owed to Étienne? The issue remained suspended for a while. Then reality had to be acknowledged: The honeymoon *à trois* was over. In order to act and build, Gabrielle needed a solid companion. And Arthur Capel was that companion: "For me he was brother, father, my whole family."

The transfer of power occurred without tears or scenes. It was a change of partners in the best tradition of French wit and style. With complete, natural ease, Capel simply took Balsan's place, at the same time that he advanced the funds necessary to purchase a business for Gabrielle.

△ Boy Capel. "That bold rule-breaker," as Paul Morand called him.

△ Gabrielle Chanel, on the threshold of a new life.

In the last months of 1910 Gabrielle Chanel found herself lodged with Arthur Capel in an elegant apartment on the Avenue Gabriel, and creating hats upstairs at number 21 in a street whose name would be associated with hers for half a century: the Rue Cambon. A plaque on the door read: Chanel Modes. At last Coco was an independent milliner at a professional address of her own choosing.

At first, Gabrielle had infinite difficulty adapting to the exigencies of business. She possessed little comprehension of how to deal with the pretty women who appeared for the first time and whom she knew to be clients of Reboux, Georgette, or Suzanne Talbot. These competitors, all famous, "arrived" women, had passed through the hard school of Parisian ateliers, submitted at a young age to training under a severe and demanding *première*. As a result, they knew all the subtleties of the trade. This was certainly not the case with Gabrielle Chanel, who had received no professional preparation whatever. A certain looseness prevailed in that first boutique, where the comings and goings proved enormously intriguing to a tradition-minded public. Sometimes it was the handsome Boy, sometimes Léon de Laborde, and then again it could be Balsan who dropped in to say *bonjour*.

Unable to cope with the idea of a *modiste* pursued by so many men, the great ladies did not return. Chanel insisted that it took a long while for her to become aware of the curiosity she aroused: "I was extremely naïve. I hadn't the remotest notion that it was I they were looking at. I saw myself as nothing but a provincial girl like so many others. The time of the extravagant dresses I had dreamed about—the sort of dresses worn by heroines—no longer existed. I had never even had a convent uniform with a *pèlerine,* embellished with Holy Ghost or 'children of Mary' ribbons so beloved in childhood. I forgot about lace, for I knew nothing rich would become me. I had only my kid-skin coat and my poor little suits. Capel said to me: 'Since it means so much to you, I will have an English tailor remake *en élégant* what you wear all the time.'"

From this came the whole style of the shop on the Rue Cambon.

◁ One said henceforth: "Mlle Dorziat of the Vaudeville." Here hatted by Chanel.

▷ Paul Signac, *La Modiste*, 1885. Buhrle Collection, Zurich.

Chanel's first boutique

In 1912 the Théâtre du Vaudeville presented a play by F. Nozière entitled *Bel Ami* and based upon the novel by Guy de Maupassant. "A strongly applauded play," wrote the critic for *L'Illustration*, adding that "Gabrielle Dorziat acted with true and spontaneous naturalness." A more reserved judgment was that of the *Matin* reviewer, who wrote that "despite a certain talent, Mlle Dorziat had something a bit dry and strained in her playing. . . ." He signed himself "Launay," but his name was Léon Blum.

Unanimity, however, governed the opinion about Dorziat's costuming, which all critics found exquisite. She was in fact dressed by Jacques Doucet. If the beautiful Dorziat was to wear clothes from the greatest couturiers in the Rue de la Paix, why not let Chanel be the milliner? To persuade the actress, Coco sent one of their old friends from Royallieu, and little Jeanne Lery did not fail. Here was a unique opportunity, and Chanel had to grasp it. Dorziat allowed herself to be convinced, and she opened wearing hats signed "Chanel."

◁△ Gabrielle Dorziat in *Bel Ami*, coiffed in a hat by Coco Chanel, who was then making her debut as a designer for the theatre while also launching her first—modest—boutique in Paris. Chanel's large straw hat, free of garnish, completed to perfection Dorziat's splendid dress from Jacques Doucet.

First clients

In 1912 the pretty ladies who had adorned the Royallieu Sundays—the horsewomen, the high-spirited friends of Balsan—made an important place for themselves in the theatre. It was they—all of them admired, applauded, and more and more photographed for the fashion magazines—who would reveal to Paris the name of a young, unknown milliner: Gabrielle Chanel.

Taking on the three giants: Worth, Doucet, and Poiret

It was not yet known that Chanel could make dresses. Only her talent for hats had been recognized. However, the word began to circulate, and one by one a few young socialites went to Coco for help with their wardrobes. The competitiveness this aroused in the little milliner stunned everyone. She truly felt ready to take on the giants of the trade.

◁ In the *Journal des modes* Dorziat wears a hat by Chanel, May 1912.

△ Little Suzanne Orlandi, who caught the attention of Parisian gossip columnists because of her liaison with Baron Foy. Here she wears a hat from Chanel Modes and a dress created from instructions drawn up by her friend Gabrielle. It is made of black velvet, with a little collar of airy petals in white lawn. Here already was the Chanel style, in what may be her first professional dress design, 1913.

Frederick Worth, couturier to the entire *Almanach de Gotha*, once executed an order from Countess Greffulhe for a nurse's smock made of Cluny lace and designed to be worn by the Countess at her daughter's lying-in. A cloth salesman born in England, Worth had moved to France, where he branched out into making dresses and became the first dressmaker to Empress Eugénie. He was the first male designer and invented the industrialized fashion business. Jacques Doucet had begun as director of a modest lingerie shop, then became an immensely rich and successful couturier of international renown, as well as a leading art collector and friend of Cubist painters. Poiret, having started out with Doucet and then Worth, was at the apogee of his career in 1912. His Oriental style with its "hobble skirt" became all the rage.

Hatmaker to the divas

In Paris no publication before 1914 exercised greater influence than *Les Modes*, a magazine launched in 1909 from the sumptuous Hôtel des Modes as part of an exhibition to which *le Tout-Paris* had been invited. Here were assembled the creations of the couturiers and milliners,

◁ The much admired and very gifted opera singer Geneviève Vix wearing another chapeau by Chanel.

△ The Seeberger brothers, who created the first photographic agency specializing in outdoor camera work, took this picture at a Paris racetrack in 1912.

together with costly furniture and portraits of the period's most beautiful women by La Gandara and Paul Helleu.

Now, in 1912, *Les Modes* announced with great fanfare the arrival of a new hat designer: Gabrielle Chanel. Full-page reproductions illustrated the Chanel hats chosen by such young and beautiful performers as Gabrielle Dorziat and the ravishing Geneviève Vix, an opera singer then drawing full houses at the Opéra-Comique for her appearances in *Manon*, *Werther*, and *Tosca*. Vix—like Dorziat, a friend of Coco's—had many points in common with the new millinery star.

By the time the photograph seen above was published, Geneviève Vix had succeeded Gabrielle in the small apartment the latter had long occupied at 160, boulevard Malesherbes: the *garconnière* of the Balsans. All the while that Gabrielle was "protected" by Étienne Balsan, Geneviève had received the same attention from Jacques Balsan, Étienne's brother. Then, in 1920, when Chanel was living with Grand Duke Dimitri, a romance developed between Vix and Prince Kyril Narishkin, which placed both young women in the circle of émigrés from tsarist Russia. But whereas Gabrielle Chanel would never marry, Prince Narishkin made Vix his wife, and Dorziat became Countess Zoghreb.

△ Until 1905, a new dress model could be photographed only in the salon of its creator and by an "artistic photographer." Reutlinger, Félix, and Manuel immortalized the creations of the Callot sisters, Paquin, and Worth. Then, suddenly, the growing number of magazines, with all the attendant publicity such media fostered—a process that no one understood better than Paul Poiret—changed everything, giving birth to fashion journalism. But *la mode* evolved more slowly than mores. Here, in 1912, an attempt at culotte-skirts did make walking easier. But what is that under the garment? A stiff corset, a whaleboned bodice, and possibly even a padded bosom. And what about the hats? "It was grotesque," declared Chanel. "How could a brain function normally under all that?" she asked much later, her implacable irony serving to give an opinion of those monumental, overloaded, headache-producing lids.

△ At Nice and very properly dressed in muff, veil, black velvet hat, and a fitted, calf-length jacket, Coco Chanel was photographed on the Promenade des Anglais attended by her cohort of admirers: Monsieur de Yturbe, Léon de Laborde, and Étienne Balsan. The simple hat of a triumphant black—which made anachronisms of the clouds of gauze and plumes that still covered her contemporaries' heads—turned custom upside down and thus epitomized what distinguished Chanel and made her different. By now already an established milliner, she could answer the question "Who dresses you?" with a ready and unblushing "I do."

◁ Adrienne Chanel at the races in Vichy. On her, Coco tried out the hats that she would later place on the heads of her clients. Half a century later Chanel would say to Paul Morand: "The women I saw at the races were wearing enormous deep-dish pies; but what horrified me most of all was that the hats did not fit down over the head."

A certain Caryathis

An encounter with Caryathis

A father who peddled in the street and chased skirts, a strong peasant heritage, a dressmaker mother from the Auvergne, a convent childhood—what a lot Caryathis and Chanel had in common. With a sack on his back, the father of Caryathis sold small wares from village to village. Then having become a journeyman baker, he acquired a certain fame presiding over the ovens at Larue before disappearing forever as chef on board the Transiberian Railway. Like the mother of Coco, Caryathis's mother had therefore been an abandoned wife. And the hapless Caryathis, apprenticed at age fourteen to Paquin, lived through a joyless childhood. Was it their common past that drew Coco to Caryathis, or the desire to know a liberated woman?

It was something quite different. A character dancer, Caryathis identified herself with the "eurythmic school" of Jaques-Dalcroze. Now, Caryathis took Chanel as a pupil, for in 1912 the *modiste* had succumbed to one last

△ The youthful Caryathis, who ran away from home and spent her meager earnings on riotous living. As a cancan dancer at the Bal Bullier, she joined the *vie de bohème* among the painters of Paris's Butte Montmartre.

▷ Bakst's poster for a ballet that Caryathis danced to the music of Erik Satie.

CARYATHIS

theatrical temptation, this time to dance. Coco evidently felt unfulfilled in her original ambitions for the stage. But she would have no more success among the pupils of Caryathis than she did in the basement of cafés in Vichy eight years earlier.

Caryathis, at age eighty, remembered having received Coco in her studio on the Rue Lamarck, which, in addition to her classes, had witnessed the teacher's tumultuous amours with the celebrated dancer Charles Dullin. Without the testimony of Caryathis, what would we know of the choreographic dreams of Coco Chanel, who felt the allure of a medium—eurythmic dance, the invention of Dalcroze— that would enthrall Paris and even influence Diaghilev.

△ About the time Chanel and Caryathis met, Colette was making her way in the tough school of music hall. Divorced from Willy, her hair cut short, and flouting every propriety in the mime-dramas produced by Georges Wague, she came in for the most scathing criticism Parisian society could offer. Another *déclassée*, however, had preceded Colette in her revolutionary path—Caryathis, the dancer who shocked her contemporaries when, in a fit of rage, she left most of her hair hanging on a nail. With this act of revenge, against a man whose ardor she had failed to arouse, Caryathis became one of the first women to appear in public sporting bobbed hair.

The beautiful *excentrique* and her friends

How can one explain Caryathis? Was she simply a primitive with excessive ambitions, or was she deliberately absurd, a very funny woman? Her name will always be linked with *La Belle Excentrique*, a ballet she danced with bare stomach and only a velvet heart over her sex. Erik Satie had written the scenario and composed the music, all in three scenes: *La Marche franco-lunaire*, *Le Mystérieux Baiser dans l'oeil*, and *Le Cancan grand-mondain*. And it was Satie who, with Carya, solicited costume designs from the painters. "My music requires extravagance and a woman more like a zebra than a deer," he said. Masked and dressed by Jean Cocteau, Caryathis danced *La Belle Excentrique*, costumed like "a madwoman from beyond the seas."

△ The painter Juan Gris and his young wife in their Bateau-Lavoir studio about 1913.

Montmartre: the capital of art

In Montmartre, the capital of art in the pre-World War I era, stood a dilapidated, moldy old tenement—mockingly called the Bateau-Lavoir after the laundry barges anchored in the Seine—that would become a veritable tinderbox for the artistic explosion known as Cubism. Here lived Picasso, Gris, Modigliani, and Jacob, a few men "all by themselves, with no support other than their own keenness and daring, whose struggle other hostile men stood back and watched. . . ." These words came

△ A portrait bearing this dedication: "For Pierre Reverdy, his friend Picasso, 15.11.21."

from Pierre Reverdy, a poet and fellow denizen of the Bateau-Lavoir. Passionately excited over the artists' innovations and himself a precursor of the new poetry, Reverdy later wrote: "I pity those who, having lived through that marvelous period, failed to participate in it, sharing its often disheartening and painful trials, its incomparably powerful emotions, its spiritual felicity. I doubt that there has ever been so much blue sky and sun in the entire history of art, or so much responsibility heroically assumed. . . ."

These lines of Reverdy allow us to measure how much he made Cubism his own. And, on the shelves of Chanel's library, the complete works of Reverdy, in their sumptuous bindings, read like a confession.

△ *Nord-Sud,* the review that Reverdy created and edited, influenced the poetic sensibility of his time as decisively as did the experiments of Reverdy's friends the Cubists. So influential was the review that Joan Miró gave the title *Nord-Sud* to a still life that he painted in Barcelona in 1917, before he had ever been to Paris or met Pierre Reverdy.

▷ Reverdy at the Bateau-Lavoir in 1912. Ardent and sensitive, Reverdy, between 1920 and 1924, had an affair with Chanel that was marked by violent quarrels and reconciliations. But even after their break-up, Reverdy, who had warm admiration for Coco, never ceased to feel a lively friendship for her.

II. Gabrielle Chanel

"Chanel built her wardrobe in response to her needs,
just the way Robinson Crusoe built his hut. . . ."
Paul Morand

The revolutionary clothes
of Gabrielle Chanel

1913: Chanel invents sports fashion

The pleasures of the Normandy coast about 1913—available only to the well-to-do. For the working classes, such recreations belonged to the realm of fantasy. The pleasure-seekers did not so much bathe as flounder about, doing so despite the fact that clothing inhibited even this much activity. One went to Étretat as if to a city, dressed from head to toe. Chanel was right: "1914 was still 1900, and 1900 was still the Second Empire."

Because in 1913 women had neither fashions nor even clothing for sports, and because her contemporaries, as she phrased it, "attended sporting events the way women in hennins attended medieval tournaments," Chanel would invent a whole new style, for relaxation and outdoor living. "Chanel built her wardrobe in response to her needs, just the way Robinson Crusoe built his hut," wrote Paul Morand in *L'Allure de Chanel*. Actually, she held onto some old-fashioned ideas, the better to adopt forms until then considered too common for fashion, such as work clothes and fatigues.

▷ Here Chanel took her inspiration from the clothing worn by Norman fishermen. The outer garment she models was made of tricot, a material never before used in fashion because it seemed totally unsuitable for tailoring—too poor and soft, good only for underwear. Chanel's creative urge was subversive, for it rejected ceremony and all its oppressiveness.

overleaf: Deauville on the eve of world conflict. The beach was left for maids and children, who had permission to make mud pies. The sea existed only to be looked at. One man even wears a top hat.

34. D

UVILLE — *La Plage*

Some ten months before war broke out, Gabrielle Chanel, financed by Boy Capel, decided to open her first boutique and to do it in Deauville. The exact location was Rue Gontaut-Biron, a chic street par excellence. Chanel employed a pair of assistants who were only sixteen and hardly knew how to sew. No matter! The new couturière set to work. The shop offered hats, to which very shortly their designer would add jumpers, jackets, and the *marinière*, or "sailor blouse," that became *the* wartime garment of all well-dressed ladies.

△ The first photograph of a couturière named Chanel, standing in front of her first boutique and wearing clothes signed by herself. Linen skirt, sailor blouse, open collar, and simple hat—all her first official creations. On the left, Adrienne, also dressed by Chanel and a living advertisement for the designer.

▷ Adrienne Chanel with her dogs on the Deauville boardwalk.

The Chanel ladies launch a style

Every day Adrienne went to the Chanel boutique, borrowed dresses and hats, different ones each time and, by

△ The lady with the greyhound, caricatured by Sem.

◁ Antoinette and Adrienne Chanel. Arm in arm and wearing creations taken from Gabrielle's boutique, the Chanel women promenaded along the pier at Deauville. They always returned triumphant, trailing admirers who talked only of the ladies' stylishness. The shop was off to a splendid start.

showing herself around town, not only became the object of great attention but also helped double Coco's business. Thanks to Adrienne, Chanel came to understand the power of mannequins. Soon her younger sister, Antoinette, was pressed into service. The Chanel sisters proved to be very popular.

An unexpected ally: Sem

The famed and feared caricaturist Sem was, if one can believe Jean Cocteau, "a ferocious insect, badly shaved, wrinkled, progressively taking on the tics of the victims he pursued. His fingers, his stump of a pencil, his round glasses, the onionskin tracings that he tore up and superimposed, his forelock, his umbrella, his dwarfish, stable-boy silhouette—all seemed to shrink into and concentrate upon his eagerness to sting." Suddenly in 1913, Sem decided to aim at a new target: high fashion. The first fascicle in a series of albums entitled *Le Vrai et le Faux Chic* (*True and False Chic*) appeared in March 1914, sowing

panic throughout the fashion salons. The lady with the greyhound was an example of "true" chic. And the woman seen by Sem as the very model of elegance was none other than Forsane, a famous demimondaine, a player at the fifty-Louis table in the casino, whose fashion consultant proved to be Chanel. *Vrai chic* therefore meant the taste of Chanel. The creators of *faux chic* had their new models presented to music and made the mannequins adopt grotesque hip-shot poses, all designed to seduce a clientele whose own demeanor and dress were of an extreme pomposity.

A caricature by Sem sometimes had the effect of launching a career. This was the case when Sem drew Chanel in the arms of a centaur Boy Capel brandishing at the end of his polo mallet a toque in the latest fashion (opposite). The allusion could not be misconstrued: If Boy was Coco's lover, he was also the financial backer of her business. Chanel had the good sense to see the advantage of Sem's charge. And the caricaturist joined the ranks of her admirers.

△ This caricature won the great humorist Sem many violent and long-lasting enmities.

▷ Polo at Deauville, where Boy Capel was top player. Coco went riding with her collar open, which, seeming rather careless, created a scandal.

▽ Goursat, or Sem, caricatured by himself.

Gabrielle Chanel now became a young woman to watch. But her celebrity was based on very little. Others might be famous by reason of their wealth or their extravagance. When it came to Chanel, however, one simply said: "She is like nobody else." Her clients were neither those ranked by Sem among the victims of *faux chic* nor those "martyred by couturiers and mad milliners" who drove the great caricaturist to indignant comparisons: "Ah, what fools! Ah, what hats! Nothing has been omitted and nothing transformed—flower pots, lampshades, casseroles, every conceivable kind of lid. They tried everything and dared everything," Sem confided to *L'Illustration* in the March 28, 1914 issue.

△ Here, at the polo grounds in Deauville, Coco makes a face at Léon de Laborde, a member of the group of dandies without whom she was rarely seen.

△ Once more, Chanel stands apart
from the crowd by virtue of the
astonishing simplicity of her attire,
an almost masculine *tailleur* made of
white linen, completely unadorned by
jewelry. No less spare is the hat, with
its relatively discreet brim and its utter
lack of "garnish." One can imagine the
effect Coco had in town, dressed in
such a radically new manner. And what
can one think of Comte de Laborde's
tweed cap? Worn at polo! And the way
he had of flirting with his cigarette
between his lips. Two chairs away, a
lady transports a good two pounds of
muslin roses on her head, and on her
bosom three cascading ropes of pearls.
Fashion also demanded that women
endure shoes with pointed toes and
triple straps that could be fastened
only with the aid of a buttonhook. How
Chanel hated all that! The talent of
Gabrielle Chanel grew strong from
swimming against the current.

Innovation vs tradition

During the beautiful weather of June 1914 Chanel saw an opportunity for real change. It now seemed possible that women might be persuaded to go bathing. And so Paul Morand noticed ladies fishing for prawns wearing "a boater embellished with Chantilly violets," as well as others who ventured into the water clad in stockings or a hat attached with a strap. In a characteristic move, Coco borrowed the material of Boy's sweaters, a technique she would often repeat in subsequent years, searching through the wardrobes of her lovers for elements of masculine attire. Thus was born a very chaste bathing suit.

◁ Chanel ready to swim in July 1914.

△ That summer, swimming for women was a fashion that caught on only with difficulty. One hesitated . . . .

▷ Sorolla y Bastida, *Promenade on the Beach.* Sorolla Museum, Madrid.

◁ The *Comœdia* reporters in 1914: Guillaume Apollinaire and the artist André Rouveyre.

August 1914

By this time all foreigners had left the French capital, except for Mrs. Moore, an American snob almost unique in the annals of Paris. Every automobile had been requisitioned, and a surcharge had been added to the price of gasoline.

At the Deauville racetrack, no one but old men and little boys dressed in huge *jean-barts* ("Buster Brown" hats) and knee britches. Also, a lone young woman. That was Gabrielle, from head to toe in Chanel. She wore a loosely fitting *tailleur*. Until then, fashion had taken as its sole purpose the accentuation of women's physical charms—and that sometimes to the point of caricature. Create a suit that would eliminate the need for a corset? A garment under which the body was merely suggested? This is what Gabrielle dared to do. She was convinced that by cultivating the natural, she would not suppress femininity—quite the opposite. The reception women gave her work confirmed this. As the guns of August began to sound, Chanel realized her first big commercial success in the world of haute couture.

What would become of her in Deauville? Who would want couture at this time? Boy, now in uniform, urged her to stay put and, above all, not to close her shop. On August 23, 1914, due to the German victory at the battle of Charleroi, that advice assumed dramatic relevance.

The Failed Festival

Another foreigner had fled Deauville. He was a Russian national with a Polish name. Much too poor to afford a vacation, he had taken up journalism in the hope of paying his way at resorts. A widely read publication recruited him to report on the scene at Deauville, with the result that when a general mobilization was announced, the new journalist found himself in the gaming room at the casino. The envoy of *Comœdia* had been born Wilhelm de Kostrowitzky, but it was under the name Apollinaire that the foreigner became known as a French poet. He called his Deauville report "La Fête manquée," and it was the work of a conscientious journalist. This was the moment when, as his Cubist friends were incorporating fragments of letters and newspapers into their paintings, Apollinaire began to compose his first "calligrammes." The night of his return to Paris in 1914 inspired him to write a poem in which the words formed the outline of a small automobile: "I shall never forget that nocturnal trip when no one spoke a word to us." He abandoned Deauville—where Chanel remained, clinging to her boutique like a shipwreck victim.

Chatelains with summer houses in Deauville sought refuge there, making the seaside resort the aristocratic city it had been in time of peace. Women needed to be able to move about on foot, to walk rapidly, and without encumbrance. This made the Chanel outfit the dress of the moment. A veritable salon developed in the shade of the great awning protecting the entrance to the Chanel boutique. The little milliner had become a commanding lady.

△ A photograph in the local press captured the image of this familiar habituée of the paddock, a young woman whose sartorial tastes went so utterly against the tendencies of the day.

◁ *Comœdia*, August 1, 1914. An article by Apollinaire with illustrations drawn by André Rouveyre.

A dying world

War? In Deauville no one could believe it. Still, the distant reality did have an effect on the outward forms of local existence. The deliberate ostentation, the obligatory display of wealth, pleasure pursued as a duty—all that would be swept away.

As Chanel would express it: "A world was dying, while another was being born. I was there, an opportunity came forward, and I took it. I was the same age as the new century, and it was to me that it looked for sartorial expression. . . . The paddock before '14! I had no doubt that while at the races, I was in attendance at the death of luxury, at the demise of the 19th century, and also at the end of an era."

August 1914 was the time of the invasion. German troops entered France at Saint-Quentin on the 27th, and on the 28th a dramatic communiqué informed the French people just how massive the attack had been: "From the Somme to the Vosges. . . . " Magnificent châteaux were destroyed: Tilleloy and Anisay burned and reduced to

△ In actuality, war was the onset, after a fourteen-year delay, of the final death agony of a stubbornly long-lived 19th century. But even this hardly seemed evident at Deauville. How could one believe that the world was really coming to an end? The end of the long afternoons spent making social calls, of taking tea at the polo grounds, of glorious entrances at the races, where women presented themselves—all sumptuousness and delicacy—wearing dresses whose maintenance was the despair of their maids.

ashes. The beautiful people who had inhabited the pala-
tial country houses appeared at Deauville, tearfully telling
how "they had lost everything." And it was true. Still, they
retained the means to reconstitute their wardrobes. This
took them to the only boutique that had not closed its
doors: *chez* Chanel.

In early September the Germans ceased to be *les
allemands* and became *les boches*. Meanwhile, the
French government abandoned Paris for Bordeaux. The
front collapsed. At Deauville a new wave of refugees
flowed in from yet more châteaux, mainly those in
Seine-et-Oise. With the enemy forces only thirty kilometers away, Parisians were fleeing. This gave Deauville
its last influx of the wealthy dispossessed. Chanel no
longer knew where to seat her clients. What a curious
fate, that a Frenchwoman should owe the Germans the
opportunity to improve her business and make herself
known beyond anything that would have been possible
in Paris.

△ In Paris, men left for the front
singing: "Long live the tomb! Death is
nothing."

125

Facing the helmeted gentlemen,
an old man in a soft hat

During the last months of 1914 the French army began its long immersion in the mud of the trenches. In Paris, meanwhile, businessmen saw their opportunity. Cloth and coal, having become scarce, came in for incredible speculation. Boy Capel, although in uniform, seized on the slightest pretext to make whirlwind visits to Paris, where Chanel had returned. He came to see her, but also to supervise his interests in coal freighters.

Now, in whatever he undertook, Boy could count on an important ally: Georges Clemenceau. The friendship that linked them provided a rather unwelcome surprise for all who had been offended by the verbal thrusts and stormy brusqueness of the old Président du Conseil. In the eyes of Boy, the clubmen, and all the young lions in general, Clemenceau was nothing but an old boor. According to every right thinker, he consisted of nothing but flaws, the worst being that he believed neither in the sovereignty of

△ At Mézières, in Bayard Square, the Crown Prince of Germany, who took great pride in his form-fitting tunics.

the Pope nor in the power of the Tsar. Was this common, uncouth man a friend worthy of Boy? But the doubts that the pugnacious politician aroused served only to reinforce Boy in his conviction that Georges Clemenceau was in fact the man of the hour. During the final months of 1914, Clemenceau, now made president of the Army Commission, became the most feared leader in France. He upbraided and harried ministers, denouncing the insufficient munitions and the delays in armaments. And he went to see for himself, going down into the trenches, dressed as if for a meeting of the Senate, except for the inevitable boots and a funny felt hat instead of his usual bowler. Clemenceau stepped up his visits to the troops, who cast their votes for him long before the population behind the lines did.

△ Clemenceau during an inspection tour of the trenches. The soldiers called him *le Vieux* ("the Old Man"). A year later, in 1917, Georges Clemenceau would govern France.

1915: lovers at Biarritz

To whom did Boy Capel owe his transfer from the army to the Franco-English wartime coal commission? Clemenceau could not have been absent when the decision was made. It placed Boy in a world that few men of that time could even have imagined—far from the menace of the first warplanes, the assault of the first tanks, the whole battle zone. It returned him to Paris and London. But before taking up his new assignment, Boy carried Gabrielle off to the Côte Basque. At Biarritz, where nothing had changed, couples danced every night, forgetting the bad times while doing the tango.

△ Boy and Gabrielle at Saint-Jean-de-Luz. With his back turned, the sugar magnate Constant Say.

△ Alfred Victor Fournier, *The Beach*.
Collection Waterhouse and Dodd,
London.

1916: a new silhouette

In wartime France one heard about those who suffered at the front, those in Paris who never ceased talking, and those in Biarritz who profited. The profiteers declared themselves eager to buy anything, by which they meant rather precisely *le luxe*. Biarritz was, of course, close to the Spanish border, and, since Spain was neutral, all sorts of shady people gathered there. A resort made fashionable by royals from all over Europe, Biarritz was the perfect setting for shopping.

It occurred to both Boy and Gabrielle that in Biarritz they could repeat the experience of the year before at Deauville, along with its happy results. Thus, a few days before his departure, Boy advanced the funds, and Gabrielle opened a *maison de couture* offering a collection of dresses priced at three thousand francs each.

Never had Biarritz seen a couturière so sumptuously installed—not in a shop but in a villa facing the casino. Chanel had her war plan. Biarritz, after all, was a sort of advanced position that put Spain within range. Neutrality and proximity made this country an excellent source of not only material but also wealthy clients. It gave the Biarritz enterprise a solid base.

Gabrielle began in July and had everything in place by September. And she did not have to wait long to discover the value of her initiative.

Orders flowed in, from the Spanish court, from Madrid, from San Sebastian, from Bilbao, etc. The Biarritz atelier was soon working at full capacity. At the end of the year, Gabrielle had achieved victory, virtually by herself, and was back in Paris. In complete command, she wanted personally to assure the liaison between her outposts. She supplied Biarritz directly, leaving her sister Antoinette in charge with full powers. In Paris, one of her ateliers worked only for Spanish clients. Now, like a general deploying his reserves according to the needs of war, Gabrielle recruited in Paris whatever personnel she lacked in Biarritz and, in a riskier maneuver, nagged Basque mothers into letting their daughters go to Paris, and this despite the zeppelins. Defeated, the mothers surrendered. Early in 1916 Gabrielle held sway over almost three hundred employees. To her surprise, she found herself able to reimburse Boy Capel, which she did without even asking his opinion. Independence at last!

◁◁ In a 1916 issue of *Harper's Bazaar* appeared the first Chanel design ever published: a dress from the Biarritz collection. Created for Antoinette's beautiful clients, it had immense allure without a trace of prewar elaborateness. Both structured bodice and high collar have been eliminated, and the garment, which is slit down the front as if by a saber, opens on a vest cut like a man's waistcoat. Instead of puffing out, the sleeves hug the arms like stockings. The hat is close-fitting and remains unburdened by the veils, plumes, and other accessories that formerly were the glory of women's headgear. As for the waist, it has disappeared, giving way to a scarf, softly slipped over the hips and left to float like a commander's sash. Surprised, but nevertheless admiring, the American editors hailed this creation with a brief caption, calling it the "charming chemise dress" of Chanel. The couturière would wait four years before receiving such a consecration in the French press. It took until 1919–20 for the country to recover its taste for frivolity.

The women's war

Mobilization paralyzed the factories of France. To reactivate industry and build up armaments, women were called into the labor force beginning in 1915. Very quickly, they constituted a full quarter of all workers in munitions factories.

In 1916 the Women's Work Committee came into being by decree of the Undersecretary of State for Artillery and Munitions. Now women found themselves inundated with opportunity. At last, they received decent pay, and on their behalf attempts were made to improve factory equipment.

It was the men, however, who, on their return from war, became the chief beneficiaries of these advances, as the

△ Édouard Vuillard, *An Armament Factory: The Forge*, 1916–17. Musée de l'Orangerie, Paris.

women found themselves dispatched back to the kitchen just as soon as hostilities had ceased. Their salaries also fell back to where they had been before the war.

Still, an important new stage had been reached, since the induction of women into the war effort initiated the whole process of liberation. This amounted to more than a mere crisis of conscience over the effectiveness of female performance in all the industries serving the army. Indeed, it was much more than that—the access that women at last gained to work that until then had been reserved for men. Nothing thereafter could prevent the progressively expanding presence of women in a great number of professions.

A subject hardly to be expected from the master of bourgeois intimacy and charm, this canvas is one of two that Édouard Vuillard painted in an armaments factory near Lyon. After he was made painter to the army in 1916, Vuillard carried his assignment all the way into the heavy, sad penumbra, the tangle of metal girders, the network of belts in the Venissieux factory directed by Thadée Natanson, the painter's best friend and founder of *La Revue blanche*. In 1917 a female worker turns shell casings in a dramatic environment.

Les Dernières Créations de la Mode

Les tissus de laine sont très souples. — Beaucoup de taffetas de fantaisie. — Le jersey est encore à la mode.

ET voilà les nouveaux tissus! Les nouveaux chapeaux! Les nouvelles robes! Cet essaim de nouveautés, cet amas de surprises ensoleille pour nous les heures mornes de février. Il semble, à manier toutes ces robes nouvelles, ces foulards adorablement fleuris, que les beaux jours d'été soient proches, les beaux jours pendant lesquels nous ne serons pas "rationnés" de soleil... Et je vais parcourir joyeusement avec vous les gammes des tissus, depuis la gabardine jusqu'à l'organdi.

Tout est souple ou presque : les beaux lainages très fins et très légers tombent en plis moelleux,... un peu d'apparence veloutée, quelques étoffes *peignées*, d'un aspect très chaud sans l'être... Dans les domaines des soieries, nous retrouvons les véritables soies d'été, le joli foulard aux mille dessins, la toile de soie, le shantung, le satin souple et le taffetas. Ceci est une surprise apportée par les

Channel.

nouveaux "paniers" que l'on essaie de relancer, ou tout au moins par les draperies des robes-tonneaux.

Et puis voici des linons, des crêpes imprimés, car nous sommes tout à *l'impression*, pour les soieries comme pour les lainages, et, naturellement, avant tout, à l'impression cachemire. Où ne trouvera-t-on pas ce dessin fameux, cette palme, ces coloris?... Dans une seule maison de tissus en coton, j'ai compté jusqu'à dix coloris de cachemire, du plus voyant au plus effacé. J'ai peur que nous ne nous lassions très vite de cette fantaisie qui tourne à l'obsession.

LES TISSUS DE LAINE

Chez Rodier, je veux, avant toute chose, vous mentionner leur triomphant *djersabure*... C'est un jersey plutôt épais, à grosses mailles, d'une apparence plutôt rugueuse; mais quels beaux plis souples forme ce tissu! On l'apprécie fort chez tous les Couturiers et l'on en a fait des

Channel.

Channel.

1917: Paris's permissive style

The *Gazette du bon ton* ceased publication in 1914. Its disappearance, like that of all the journals which had made French fashions known abroad, explains why the feat of walking and showing a bit more than the ankle would remain a Parisian exclusive until 1919. Only after World War I did the French become aware of the shock felt by foreign visitors when confronted with that fraction of visible leg. Yet hardly had the fashion been seen when it became universal.

In 1916 Chanel set out to find a machine-made fabric as close to knitting as possible. Rodier, in lieu of something better, showed her a material then considered unusable: jersey. But it proved to be precisely what Chanel wanted: knitting made by machine. She swore to Rodier that the fabric would take over the market.

◁ In March 1917 *Les Élégances parisiennes* made a full-page announcement of a new "fashion" fabric: jersey. Hats and dresses by Gabrielle Chanel.

△ In the same issue, three Chanel jacket-skirt ensembles made of jersey. *Les Élégances* was a publicity organ.

△◁ The photo of Hilda May on a motor scooter and in a Chanel dress appeared in the press with the following comments: "Since taxis are so rare, gas is rationed, and chauffeurs are not as abundant as one would like, perhaps the example set here by Hilda May will incite Parisian ladies to adopt this small vehicle?"

In the provinces, concern for respectability

For Adrienne Chanel, Gabrielle's aunt, the war years were something else. Her long-faithful fiancé, still hoping to obtain his parents' consent for him to marry the person he loved, dictated from the front every move that she made. Paris was out of bounds, for there the hotels were crowded, and to have a lover no longer remained an impossibility. In this permissive and patriotic society, aviators found themselves by far the most in demand.

Adrienne's protector convinced her to settle in a provincial city, in a discreet place where she could live free from

△ At Vichy an Argentinian in town for the waters, playing host to Maud on the pillion and Adrienne in the side car.

the menace of both Big Bertha and slanderous gossip. But one condition had to prevail, which was that she never be seen in public without Maud Mazuel at her side. Thus, the chaperone of the Chanel girls during their period at the Moulins café-concert, the very affable hostess of the house in Souvigny where Adrienne had met her *adoré*, became on all occasions the most loyal of followers. Finally on April 29, 1930, Adrienne married her aristicratic lover. She had waited thirty years.

△ Adrienne, Maud, and an officer on leave enjoy an outing on the River Allier near Vichy. Hats by Chanel.

Innovations that proved decisive

Gabrielle immediately adopted the new fabric made by Rodier—jersey—for herself. What she made with it—an unbelted, three-quarter-length overcoat, free of all ornament and almost masculine in its severity—dispelled the doubts of her suppliers.

But even a firm less alert than Rodier, without knowing anything at all, but responsive to what makes true feminine elegance, would have seen right away that this garment had a future and offered something highly original in its sheer freedom. Here, embellishment gave way to line, yielding a costume born of the single-minded logic of its creator. Chanel wanted to achieve what no one else had dared to do with such candor: women going forth liberated by shortened skirts and loosely fitting garments that deemphasized the bust and lower curves. Chanel imposed upon fashion a novelty so decisive that it literally brought clothing into the 20th century. As for the nostalgic ones—and there were many of them who,

◁ Dressed by Chanel, Adrienne and Antoinette at the races, accompanied by the Maharajah of Indore, who, of all the foreigners in the colony of allies, had the richest tastes. Boutet de Monvel did his portrait, showing the Indian prince full length, wearing an ample black cape lined in white satin.

△ Illustration in *Fémina*, February 1917. An ensemble made of jersey, consisting of a three-quarter-length jacket and a loose skirt, typical of those launched by Chanel.

▷△ May 1918. Gabrielle Chanel, lying in the fallow grass of a meadow, could be taken as a symbol of the year the war ended and of the discreet elegance of French women at this time. Moreover, her hat and her dress alike conceal secrets: under the first, bobbed hair; under the second, no corset whatever.

▷ Chanel standing, dressed in the same outfit.

like Marcel Proust, expressed sadness at the sight of dresses "not even made of material" and of "ordinary-looking" women. Their laments would remain futile, for nothing could revive a defunct way of dress.

Success agrees with women, and it made Chanel still more beautiful. She went from success to success. That year she had bought the Villa Larralde for her business, paying three hundred thousand francs cash. Everything worked for her, even in Paris during the worst year of the war, when the capital was menaced by a new cannon, Big Bertha, whose bombardments brought the walls of Saint-Gervais down on the Good Friday congregation.

Chanel at Uriage, in a Basque beret and bobbed hair

The year 1918 saw the awful war reaccelerate, as if four years of fierce struggle had been for nothing. Once more the Germans advanced and disaster seemed imminent. With the enemy at the gates of Paris, the well-to-do fled anew to Deauville or to Biarritz. But atrocious as it was, this dramatic crisis would in no way work against the interests of Gabrielle. As before, the war played right into her hands, for nothing could prevent its giving women what had been previously beyond their grasp: liberty.

△ A sporty woman in a Basque beret: Chanel. Five years earlier, two Englishwomen who on a windy day at Deauville had dared to adopt such a headdress found themselves accused of eccentricity.

The great novelty was that women no longer had to ask permission to go wherever they wished. The worldly ones even dared to enter the Ritz bar, where access had been denied them in time of peace. Located, as chance would have it, directly across the street was Chanel's boutique, at 21, rue Cambon. Henceforth, Gabrielle would find herself on the route taken each day by women eager to know what moved and lived in a great city, where for the first time they were circulating alone and on foot. In later years, Gabrielle moved over to the Ritz where she slept when in Paris.

△ A hiker in a style never seen before, carrying a cane and wearing a thick cardigan, an ample skirt, and a long scarf. Like the whole outfit, the shoes—round-toed, white, and simple—look rather British, a quality Gabrielle would have absorbed from Boy. In another act of independence, the designer had cut her hair even shorter than in 1917.

The conversion to short hair

The bobbed-hair offensive got underway in May 1917, the date verified in the journal of Paul Morand: "For three days now the fashion has been for women to wear short hair. Everyone has adopted it, with Mme Letellier and Chanel leading the way. . . ."

Bobbed hair was shocking, irreversible, and, on the whole, grudgingly accepted. Only by means of the most absurd ruses did women get their families to tolerate the new style. Thus Colette, in order to appease her in-laws, pretended that she had accidentally overturned an oil lamp onto her loosened hair. But in sacrificing, at the instigation of her husband, Monsieur Willy, tresses measuring some 1.58 meters (about five feet), she involuntarily anticipated fashion by at least a decade. This was in 1903, when, in the company of a similarly coiffed Polaire and an opera-hatted Willy, her appearance in a theatre box created a scandal, causing Willy to be known along the boulevards as "the man with two monkeys."

△◁ The only album of drawings by Modigliani that has survived intact contains among its twenty-seven sheets this 1915 portrait of Mme Moïse Kisling, who pioneered bangs.

△ Caryathis during the run of *La Belle Excentrique*, when she too became a devotée of the scandalous coiffure à la Joan of Arc.

◁ Gabrielle Chanel in 1917, the period in which Morand noted in his *Journal d'un attaché d'ambassade* that Coco "is definitely becoming a personage."

An unheard-of audacity: sunbathing

No one but street vendors and peasants had ever been tanned. Whereas a milky skin seemed a sure sign of aristocracy, a tanned one could indicate nothing but modest or plebeian origins. This attitude had long been in effect, and, among all the innovations undertaken by Chanel, the idea of fearing the sun less would prove to be the most difficult to promote. Even Coco continued to wear gloves when out of doors, lest her hands look as if they had done manual labor. Not until 1923 could women be seen on the beach sunning themselves without even a hat for protection.

△▷ On a picnic in 1918, a bareheaded Chanel blissfully drinks in the sun's rays, while a more cautious Adrienne still wears a hat and even uses her umbrella as a parasol.

▷ It is also revealing to note that even though Chanel dared to let the sun have its way with her face, she continued to cover her hands. Gloves were essential because no woman of the world could risk having her hands look as though they had done manual labor.

Comfort: an intoxicating freedom

If feminine fashion remained beholden to Paul Poiret for
such important innovations as the softening of the corset
and a slight abridgment of skirts, and if Poiret was a col-
orist unlike anyone who came after him, it was nonetheless Gabrielle who in 1918 insisted on the right of women
to comfort and ease of movement. Everything favored it.
The notion of woman as an object or possession could
exist no longer, and the victory of the automobile over
horsedrawn carriage was an accomplished fact, bringing
about a whole new conception of how to clothe the
female body. "I set the fashion for a quarter of a century,"
said Chanel. "Why? Because I knew how to express my
own time."

△ Chanel on holiday in 1918.

146

Poiret had created a fluid style, without a cinched waist. Chanel went further and left the waist scarcely indicated. Poiret allowed the foot to appear, but Gabrielle emphasized the skirt's rise by generously freeing the ankle. In the same stroke she also eliminated the need for a certain movement that men had so voluptuously ogled: the gesture used by women to gather up their skirts in preparation for mounting a step. What else disappeared? An era in the life of women, their demands as clients to whom everything was owed; the exclusivity of fabrics and designs. Until then, it would have been the ruin of a couturier should a customer encounter another woman wearing a similar creation. In changing all that, Chanel transformed forever the look of street life.

△ From left to right: Gabrielle, Marguerite Vincent (a former dancer from the Theatre de la Monnaie), and Adrienne Chanel, all wearing variations of the same Chanel ensemble.

A certain Misia Sert

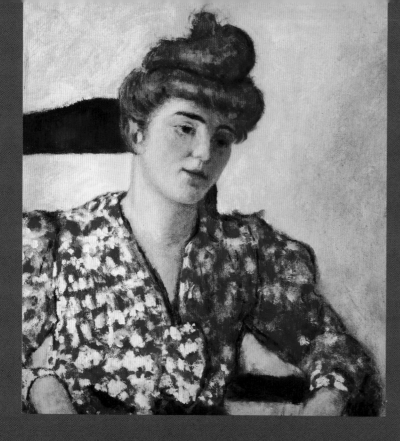

Misia, her husbands, her painters, her musicians, her poets

It was at a dinner in the home of Cécile Sorel, in 1917, that Gabrielle first met the only woman who had an undeniable (though unacknowledged) influence upon her—the only woman, in fact, to whom Gabrielle Chanel would grant any genius whatever.

Misia Sophie Olga Zénaïde Godebska was born in March 1872 in St. Petersburg. Her father was Polish and her mother half Russian and half Belgian. Even though pregnant, Mme Godebska decided to join her painter-sculptor husband in Russia, where she knew he could not be trusted among women. Having surprised him installed with a mistress, she gave birth to a daughter and died.

This left Misia to be brought up by her Russian grandmother, a spendthrift musician, and her grandfather, a violin virtuoso who taught the infant notes before she could learn the alphabet. Several stepmothers, some more sympathetic and some less so, succeeded one another until finally Misia's father decided to claim his daughter.

△ Édouard Vuillard, *Portrait of Misia Natanson*, 1897.

Together, they lived in several different Parisian houses, which, depending upon Godebski's success or lack of it, could be either modest or sumptuous. Misia detested all of them and never ceased to miss her beloved grandmother's pseudo-Italian villa. Located on the outskirts of Brussels, it was a house that simply vibrated with music, where a consumptive pianist died at the keyboard while playing Chopin, and where Liszt had come as a friend, taking a tiny Misia on his knee to play her Beethoven's Bagatelle in E-flat.

Placed in a boarding school at the Sacré-Coeur, Misia remained there six years, wildly impatient for the great day each week when she went for her piano lesson with Gabriel Fauré. Little wonder, for she was an especially gifted pupil.

At age fifteen, during summer vacation, Misia had a violent altercation with one of her stepmothers and fled to London, where, with four thousand francs borrowed from the Portuguese consul, she set up alone. That at least is the version she gave of what has remained a rather mysterious escapade. Some months later, however, Misia was back in Paris with a place in a modest building. She lived from piano lessons procured for her by Fauré. Holding his pupil in the highest esteem, the great composer predicted a career for her on the concert stage.

When Fauré learned of Misia's engagement he dissolved into tears. The pupil nonetheless married a cousin, Thadée Natanson, who was Polish-born but had become French. He was twenty, she twenty-one years old. Even though admitted to the bar, Natanson spent less time there than in artistic and literary circles. Proust, Monet, Renoir, Odilon Redon, Signac, Debussy, Mallarmé, Gide, and, most of all, the Nabis and Toulouse-Lautrec, with whom Thadée had especially strong ties, became the habitués of the young couple's salon in Rue Saint-Florentin. All the guests of that house were, without exception, sensitive to the youth, the pianistic gifts, and the charm of Misia, whose image her painter-friends—especially Édouard Vuillard, Pierre Bonnard, and Félix Valloton—recorded with an astonishing variety and abundance.

△ Photograph by Édouard Vuillard of Misia Natanson and her sister-in-law, Marthe Godebska.

▷ Édouard Vuillard, *The Two Sisters-in-Law*. Lithograph.

La revue
blanche
bi-mensuell
le nº 60 cent.
12 francs par An
1 rue Laffitte
Paris
Charpentier et Fasquelle, édite
11, rue de Grenelle

Misia and *La Revue blanche*

It was in 1889 at Spa that a group of young vacationers, among them Alexandre and Thadée Natanson, decided to found a review for the purpose of advancing new talent and ideas. What emerged was the famous *Revue blanche*, which Gide called *le centre de toutes les divergences*. While Alexandre served as director, Thadée became editor and indeed the main driving force behind the whole enterprise. After starting in Belgium, the founders soon moved their operation to Paris. Proust, Barrès, Verlaine, Fénéon, Zola, Mallarmé, Jarry, Léon Blum, Oscar Wilde, Francis Jammes, Mirbeau, Claudel, and Péguy all appeared in a journal that for twelve years came out monthly or bi-monthly and had a decisive influence on the arts and letters of the period. Posters promoting *La Revue blanche* were created by Thadée's friends—Toulouse-Lautrec, Vuillard, and Bonnard—all of whom took the editor's young wife as their favorite model. Thus, Misia, whether dressed in a high-collared black coat or in a fur wrap, muff, and veil, came to symbolize *La Revue blanche* in the eyes of the French.

△ ◁ A rare photograph of Misia Natanson wearing a coat with triple *pèlerine*.

△ Pierre Bonnard, *La Revue blanche* poster. Misia in her triple cape.

◁ Henri de Toulouse-Lautrec, *La Revue blanche* poster. Misia with her muff.

Misia, Vuillard, and the latter's Kodak

"It is a living witness," said Jacques Salomon, who evoked the period when Vuillard had just discovered photography: "Sometimes, without interrupting the conversation, Vuillard would move toward his Kodak and, steadying it on a piece of furniture (that is, on the back of a chair), would blindly aim it in the direction of the scene he wanted to capture. After a short warning—'One second, please!'—we would hear the shutter click."

Once again, Misia Natanson was the ideal model. The style of her clothes as much as of her person proved an inspiration for her friend Vuillard. The young pianist's checked cotton dress with puffed sleeves, photographed in the garden of the Relais at Villeneuve-sur-Yonne (the country house that every Sunday became the merry chapel of *La Revue blanche*), is recognizable in the lithograph where Misia stands over a checkers game. Meanwhile, her charming teagown with its velvet bow

△ Édouard Vuillard, photograph of Misia in a meadow.

△ Édouard Vuillard, *A Game of Checkers*. With Misia watching.

over the bodice has been subtly sketched in the portrait by Vuillard as well as in the wonderful lithograph that the artist made of Misia and her sister-in-law (Marthe, the wife of Cipa Godebski) engaged in a family tête-à-tête.

It should be noted, however, that Vuillard was not alone in his complicity with the camera. Bonnard too—Misia's other painter, who did the portrait of her and Thadée now in Brussels—delighted in the marvels that could be accomplished by the magical eye that science had placed at the service of art.

Misia, Thadée, Blum, and Dreyfus

"Thadée was becoming more and more preoccupied with finances," wrote Misia in her memoirs, adding: "*La Revue blanche* had heavy expenses, and year by year the deficit

became more difficult to cover." What she fails to mention is that, for all her powers as a muse, Misia hastened the ruin of Thadée Natanson. Ignorant of rules, what did she know of measure and economy? Can one forget that when she went to collect Toulouse-Lautrec in a cart at the little country station near Fontainebleau, Misia sported her most beautiful emeralds?

Confronted with insurmountable financial problems, Thadée suddenly succumbed to the vexations of his enterprise and ceded the dying *Revue blanche* to Fasquelle. He then went into coal, on behalf of a company commissioned to build a tramway system for Toulon. But

△ Photograph by Édouard Vuillard of Misia and Thadée Natanson at home in Paris, ca. 1898.

this did not prevent his throwing himself into the battle for the rehabilitation of Captain Dreyfus, raising funds to help advance the magnanimous ideas of his friend Léon Blum, enthusiastically organizing theatrical evenings that anyone could afford, and struggling to fill the coffers of the League for the Rights of Man, an organization that he helped found.

Thadée needed a Maecenas, for he himself was more than half ruined. When the benefactor appeared, he was Alfred Edwards, the newspaper magnate and founder of *Le Matin*, which had the largest circulation in France. Now the charm of Misia had its predictable effect upon Edwards, who lost no time in "saving" the husband by separating him from his wife. Thus, Thadée found himself posted as director of a coal mine in far-off Hungary. Since

◁ Félix Vallotton, *Misia on a Settee,* 1898.

▷ Félix Vallotton, *Misia at Her Dressing Table,* 1898. Musée d'Orsay, Paris.

Félix Vallotton

Félix Vallotton was as much a familiar of the Natanson household as Vuillard. In addition to the famous portrait that he did of Thadée as a young man, Vallotton executed numerous portraits of the Nabis— that is, the writers and painters of *La Revue blanche.* Vallotton also did two portraits of Misia alone. One shows the subject at her dressing table, wearing a décolleté dress and one of those velvet bows that gave such joy to painters. The other has her posed upon an upholstered settee, looking somewhat like a doll. Even though Misia's face reveals an undeniable hardness, the two portraits depart from Vallotton's usual pessimistic, even fierce handling.

An artist very much closed in upon himself, Vallotton confided to his journal: "What has man done that is so bad that he must submit to this terrifying associate called 'woman.'" But, when faced with the couple that Thadée formed with his young wife, even Vallotton melted, grew tender, and ceased to be the painter who Jules Renard said "feasted only on bitterness."

money meant nothing to him but the means of serving the cause of nascent socialism and the League of the Rights of Man, Thadée strove to make the working conditions of his labor force consistent with his social ideals. He even went into debt in order to build a workers' city; indeed, he committed the last of his resources to this undertaking.

When the inevitable disaster finally occurred, Edwards, who had done nothing to prevent it, stepped forward. He agreed to advance the funds that were most immediately required, but with one condition—that Misia be his. This was how the beautiful Misia Natanson, having agreed to be the stake in this game, divorced Thadée and, on February 24, 1905, in Paris, became the rich Madame Edwards.

The beautiful Madame Edwards

Edwards had been born in Pera, the European quarter of Constantinople, of a father who, as physician to the Sultan's harem, had accumulated a considerable fortune. Although horribly jealous—"the jealousy of a Turk," said Misia—Edwards managed to agree that Misia should continue to see her painter friends. It was in her beautiful apartment on the Rue de Rivoli that Misia posed for the nearly paralyzed Renoir, whose large portrait shows his subject dressed in pink.

A few years later, Maillol wanted her to pose for him. "Beauty should be copied wherever it is found," he wrote to her. "Quite naturally, therefore, I address myself to you." The sculptor saw her as an immortal figure, but she refused to pose.

△ Édouard Vuillard, *Misia against Flowered Wallpaper*, 1898.

◁ Misia in 1908, followed by her husband, Alfred Edwards, the owner of *Le Matin* and the principal shareholder in *Le Figaro*. "I was among the first to own one of those engines born of the brains of Messieurs de Dion, Bouton, Panhard, and Levassor, which could achieve a speed of thirty kilometers per hour," wrote Misia proudly in her memoirs, published posthumously in 1952. "It was not without a slight shudder that one climbed upon the foldout runningboard so as to wedge oneself into the upholstered seats."

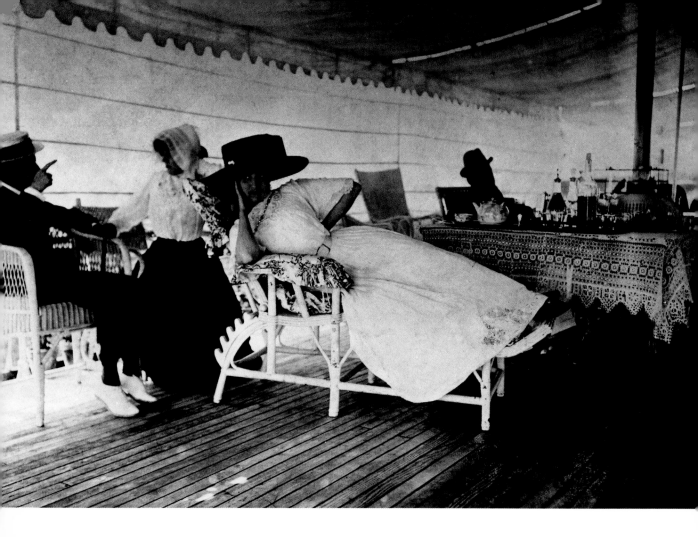

△ Misia Edwards on board the
Aimée, in the company of Sem and
Lucienne Bréval.

Edwards owned a château, a real one with keep, battlements, and all the rest. Misia would not stop until she had persuaded him to sell it. "I have always had a horror of châteaux," she revealed in her memoirs. "Landed property has never meant anything to me. Why should I restrict myself to five or six hundred acres when I can enjoy the entire world?" Hardly had the château been sold when Misia asked Edwards to have a boat constructed.

It was a houseboat called the *Aimée*, measuring thirty-five meters in length. But the cordiality between Misia and Edwards did not last long. It dissolved when he left her for a beautiful demimondaine: Lanthelme. This new relationship, however, had a tragic and mysterious end: Lanthelme jumped into the Rhine from the bridge of the *Aimée*. To say the least, the affair did great damage to Edwards, and in 1909 he and Misia were divorced.

The great Misia Sert

If Misia Godebska's second marriage developed her taste for luxury, it was a third union, in 1914, this time with the bearded Catalan painter José-Maria Sert, that marked the beginning of her public fame. From that time forward, no artistic manifestation occurred without the involvement of the influential Misia. A friend of Diaghilev, of the dancers he promoted, of the choreographers, designers, and musicians he discovered, Misia became associated with every one of the impresario's creations. What a destiny! This inspirational force, this counselor who for fifty years lived among the greatest artists of her time, making herself indispensable to them, actually was a person of no culture whatever. "She never opened a book," said Chanel. "She does not even read her mail!" Which was true.

△ A drawing by Jean Cocteau of Misia at Monte Carlo in 1911, at the time of the first performance of the ballet *Le Spectre de la rose*. With her are José-Maria Sert, Jean Cocteau, and Sergei Diaghilev.

165

△ Édouard Vuillard, *Misia at Her Piano*, ca. 1898.

Misia according to . . .

Mallarmé

Aile que du papier reploie
Bats toute si t'initia
Naguère à l'orage et la joie
De son piano Misia.

Reverdy

I love you so much. I think of you with such tenderness. You cannot imagine how or how much. Sometimes one of your phrases, or a word that you have spoken to me, echoes in my heart, and then this sweetness mingles with the bitterness of not being able to embrace you, or place my hand upon yours, or even see you. How often have I cursed the obstacles that separated us—my excessive sensitivity, our social differences, my stupidity among people whom I should have suffered just to see you live. You have occasionally reproached me for not coming to see you more frequently. But you could not realize that I would have wanted to isolate you too exclusively, thereby sacrificing everything at once! My dear, tenderly beloved friend, please understand that into my life, which never ceases to be a mute torment, you have brought something substantial—happiness and also suffering—because it is true that one cannot truly love without suffering, and you are among those whom I love to the point of pain. My arms, my lips, heart all long for you. You are part of my life. A blue side. . . .

Cocteau

One must extol a bit those warmblooded and deep women who live in the shadows of great men and who, from the margins of artistic creation, have a mysterious effect merely by generating ringlike waves more beautiful than necklaces. It is impossible to visualize the golden ceilings of José-Marie Sert, the sunfilled world of Renoir, Bonnard, Vuillard, Roussel, Debussy, and Ravel, the prophetic spotlight of Lautrec, the prism of Verlaine, and the radiant dawn of Stravinsky without seeing the figure of a young ribbon-striped tiger, its face as sweet and cruel as a pink cat, which was Misia the evening she wore Scheherazade's egret and sat enthroned at the center of the royal box at the Ballets Russes, filling the theatre and the violent dancing with her own fluid presence, just as she once did the light-spangled gardens of the Impressionists. Yes, it is in the fur-and-silk envelope with which Paul Poiret and Paul Iribe wrapped their sultanas, presiding as the godmother of the light-footed troupe of Sergei Diaghilev, that we see and recognize our friend. Her fan bears Mallarmé's famous quatrain, and I do believe that out of all her marriage contracts, all her residence permits, the poem is probably the sole piece of identification kept by this admirably disordered Polish woman, in whom whole fortunes and the compliments of P.-J. Toulet and P. Vuillard have been sunk. Between short stays in apartments that she decorates and then abandons as if they were mere perches, Madame Sert lives on the top floor of the Hôtel Meurice.

When I became her friend, she had just left the hotel for a sort of lantern high over the Quai Voltaire. The salon was illuminated on the north by green light, by the Seine on the south, and in orange by the canvases of Bonnard. Misia herself had cut these canvases in order to make them fit the exact configuration of the walls. Call it a scandal! We have dogeresses and great priestesses. We have muses; indeed, we have them to give away. But how much more rare and indispensable to the arts, which risk growing too fat, are those ultrafemale women who bring havoc—the spirit of dressmaking and scissors—into the temple.

"The angels fly," wrote Chesterton, "because they take themselves lightly." Out of love, not out of disrespect, Misia continually kneads the dough and keeps it from hardening. Only strong artists who fear their role as idols benefit from this iconoclast, as she whips life like a top, getting drunk on its hum, and never allowing speed to become stationary.

There we are face to face with one of those women to whom Stendhal granted genius. The genius to go forward, to laugh, to put things in their place, to make with the fan, to climb into a carriage, to invent a crown. It is a genius that Misia possessed to such a degree that in writing *Thomas l'Imposteur,* I could try as I might to project my mind all the way to the San Severina, but Misia automatically became, whatever the cost, the model for the Princesse de Bornes.

Morand

Misia ("She was twenty years old when I saw her at her father's house," said my father, "a beautiful panther, imperious, bloodthirsty, and idle"). Misia, not as her weak *Mémoires* suggest, but as she was in actuality: bubbling with joy or fury, original and derivative, collector of geniuses, all of them in love with her: Vuillard, Bonnard,

Renoir, Stravinsky, Picasso . . . collector of hearts and of Ming trees made of rose quartz, launching her fancies, which became the fashion as soon as they were caught by her followers, taken up by journalists, and imitated by stylish ladies with empty heads. Misia, queen of modern baroque, having wrapped her life in the bizarre, in mother-of-pearl. Misia sulking, artificial, bringing together friends who did not know one another, "the better to mix them up later on," as Proust put it. Ingenious in her perfidy, refined in cruelty, Misia, to whom Philippe Berthelot said one dared not entrust what one loved: "Here is a cat, so hide your birds," he would say as she knocked at his door. In her *boutique fantasque* on the Quai Voltaire, she stimulated genius the way certain kings succeed in creating military heroes, merely by the vibrations of her own existence, by some invisible oscillation of her hazel branch. Misia, tough as the life bolted down inside her, avaricious, generous, spender of millions, cajoler, brigand; crafty, commercial, more Madame Verdurin than the original, prizing and despising men and women at first glance. Misia of Symbolist Paris, of Fauve Paris, of Paris in the time of the Versailles Treaty, of the Paris in Venice. Misia, as upholstered as a sofa, but if you hope for rest, a sofa that could send you to the devil. Never satisfied, Misia, whose piercing eyes laughed even as the mouth pouted.

In this sickened gourmand, disgust followed rapture, as no succeeded yes, and thunder, lightning. With her, one had to be quick.

Chanel

We like people only for their faults and Misia has given me ample and numerous reasons to like her. Misia sticks by only what she does not understand; meanwhile, she understands almost everything. I have remained a mystery to her, which explains a loyalty that, while always crazy, recovers—after certain lapses—its constancy. She is a rare being, who can please only women and a few artists. Misia is to Paris what the goddess Kali is to the Hindu pantheon—the goddess of both destruction and creation. She kills and spreads her germs without knowing it. Satie called her "Mother Kill-All" and Cocteau "the Maker of Angels." This is unjust. Certainly Misia does not create, but in some twilight areas she does the useful and beneficent work of a phosphorescent larva.

It cannot be denied that in her the genius is unconscious, but the Asiatic love of destruction and of sleeping after a catastrophe, her soul calm in the midst of ruin, clearly present in that *polonaise*.

Misia has no sense of measure. The "French clarity of reason" and the "blue line of gentle hills" mean nothing to this nomad of the steppes.

Misia—from the time she was fifteen years old, ever since Valvins, where with hair and sleeves rolled up she posed the brothel girls for Toulouse-Lautrec, Renoir, Vuillard, and Bonnard, all the way to Picasso, Stravinsky, and Diaghilev—has lived fifty years among the greatest artists, and yet she has no culture. She has never opened a book.
—"Take this book, Misia."
—"Why? I wonder how you find the time to read."
She doesn't even read her mail.

▷ Édouard Vuillard, *Misia Sert*, 1915.

The death of Boy Capel

It was in 1919 that touring by automobile caught on, especially among the affluent who could afford a chauffeur. Boy Capel became one of the first victims among those said to be afflicted by a "contagious madness." The handsome Boy was killed on December 24 of that year. A news agency dispatch gave the facts: "Captain Capel was traveling from Paris. He was on his way to Cannes when a tire on his automobile blew out." With the death of Boy, the killer car cut a bloody path into high society. The tragic event left Chanel broken and, for once, incapable of masking the immense sorrow that she felt. She was, in fact, mourning Boy for the second time, the first having occurred in 1918, when, for reasons of his own personal ambition, he married Lady Diana Wyndham, which made him the brother-in-law of Lord Lovat. It was Chanel's friends José-Maria and Misia Sert who undertook to restore her will to live. This brought Gabrielle into the circle of artists where Misia reigned. Now the couturière gained the authority that allowed her, in subsequent years, to appreciate and defend talents that were as diverse as they were original.

The sport of automobiles

The year 1919 marked the renewal of the sport of automobile driving after the interruption caused by World War I. Although the lack of materials was cruelly felt, racing recommenced with professional drivers, many of them now fighter-plane veterans, redoubling their daring. This was certainly true of the famous Eddie "Rick" Rickenbaker, the American ace of the French flying forces—and André Boillot, who in 1919 won the dangerous Targa Florio in Sicily. That year, twenty-one contestants made their start in abominable weather and along roads that had been transformed into sloughs. The test, consisting of four times around 1500 turns and over a mountainous circuit 800 kilometers long, produced a brutal contest. The press remarked on the "mad temerity" of Boulot who, pushed by Ascari, brushed precipices, scraped rocks, ground down masses of stone, and skidded over mountain snows. Ascari, just when he had broken the record for this course, disappeared into a ravine. As for Boillot, he was in sight of the goal when some spectators surged onto the roadway, protesting the victory of a foreigner. Boillot had no choice but to slam on the brakes and, after a triple spin, finally crossed the finish line—backward! The spirited presence of the American journalist W. F. Bradley, a passionate admirer of French pilots and airplane builders, saved Boillot from disqualification. Bradley quickly implored the French driver to restart his motor and make a second pass over the line, this time front first. Exhausted, Boillot complied, with the jeers of the mob ringing in his ears. Shouting "C'est pour la France!" he fainted. Just then two Italians arrived—Gambori and Mariando—but it was too late. The unconscious Boillot was declared the winner. His race, now a legend in Sicily, has remained one of the most extraordinary feats in the annals of the automobile.

△ Serious accident in the south of France.

▷ Spring 1919, Gabrielle Chanel en route to Biarritz.

Avec stupeur, j'appris de la bouche de Bienvenu, que les obus peuvent fleurir sans l'aide de cette bienfaisante pluie: la musique patriotique.
(Moi, qui sais de la guerre ce qu'en sait un habitué des cinémas!)

Aid for a child of the century: Radiguet

Raymond Radiguet belonged to the generation that had been deprived of its fathers by the war but that had not itself endured the hell of the trenches. Radiguet's precocity as well as his rage to live aroused both fear and indignation. Max Jacob, who had discovered Radiguet in 1918 and had introduced him to Cocteau and then to Misia, described the youth: "He was handsome, he was grave. He had, it seemed, read everything. He was imperturbable. He could be seen almost every night sitting at Le Boeuf sur le Toit. Radiguet drank a considerable amount, but his face, his heavy mouth, his stubborn eyebrows remained absolutely immobile."

It should be remembered that he was hardly fourteen years old when he wrote his first poem, "Les Joues en feu"; that he was seventeen when his masterpiece, *Le Diable au corps*, transformed this enfant terrible into a monster in the eyes of those whom the novel scandalized. It must also not be forgotten that he died while only twenty, of a badly treated typhoid infection, leaving incompleted *Le Bal du*

△ Manuscript by Raymond Radiguet entitled *In Memoriam*, written ca. 1919. He was then sixteen years old.

◁ Roger de La Fresnaye, drawing of Raymond Radiguet, April 1921.

comte d'Orgel, which came out after the author's death. Finally, we should remind ourselves that it was Chanel whom Cocteau called when it became necessary to transport the fever-racked Radiguet from his hotel room to a Paris hospital. She paid all the medical bills, while Misia arranged the funeral.

In his memoirs, Georges Auric states that he was one of the few people, if not the only one, in whom Raymond Radiguet freely confided, and describes the young author as follows: "He seemed like a child, and even in the most serious moments he did not cease to appear so. . . . Hardly a talker, except with women. Right away it must be stated that he was the exact opposite of a homosexual, and if he had lived three months longer, he would have married." Auric also reveals him living like someone who was counting his days. From bar to bar, from girl to girl, the young disciple of Jean Cocteau escaped him more and more.

△ Jean Oberlé, drawing of Raymond Radiguet with his passionate discoverer and promoter: Jean Cocteau.

▷ At Pramousquier, Radiguet dressed up as a dowager. For a hat he wears a lampshade, with his umbrella made from a broomstick.

174

Paris, where nothing was as before

The world of Marcel Proust is dead, and we are in the time of Radiguet. Just as fashionable events changed in spirit, so the *grands seigneurs* changed their style, and the great "locomotives" of the Belle Époque lost out in their hope of reviving the prewar days, when members of a class could associate only with one another. The turn-of-the-century era belonged to Comte Boni de Castellane, with his Palais Rose imitating Versailles, his extraordinary fêtes, and his frigid formality.

And 1920? It was the time of Comte Étienne de Beaumont. At his townhouse *le monde*—meaning the only "world" that counted, that of the aristocracy—mingled for the first time with exponents of nonofficial, nonacademic, un-"honored" art. Beaumont became the inventor of a new form of snobbism requiring that value take precedence over title, talent over wealth, artists over the establishment. In Beaumont's gilded boiserie salon, bordering on the Rue Masseran, Proust attended the last

△ Jacques Émile Blanche,
Portrait of Marcel Proust, 1892.
Musée d'Orsay, Paris.

soirée of his life. He was received like a sovereign. Later, whole troupes of timid young unknowns—painters, musicians, writers, poets—made themselves known and got their start in the home of Étienne de Beaumont. But the true Beaumont, who could claim to have unmasked him? Under an exterior of grandiose frivolity, he hid a lacerated sensibility. His style also provoked a good bit of ridicule, but the Count saw no other way of expressing his horror of sensible behavior.

For those of facile judgment and hasty comment, the name of the Comte de Beaumont signifies little more than an elegant manner and a lingering memory of receptions, balls, and parties of exceptional liveliness and fantasy. Happily, there are other observers. For them, Beaumont remains the sole French aristocrat—with the possible exception of the Vicomte de Noailles—who supported the new spirit; the only one whose involvement was not limited simply to encouragement.

△ Marie Laurencin (on the right), whose art now seems so childish—"Ladies' work," said Forain contemptuously, "a stitcher of shoes"—but who will forever seem sacred for having been the great passion of Apollinaire. Here she is with Nicole Groult, then a famous couturière and the wife of André Groult whose furniture designs typified the 1920s to perfection. A commission from Étienne de Beaumont for Les Soirées de Paris gave Marie Laurencin the opportunity to create the sets and costumes used in the ballet Les Roses.

In creating Les Soirées de Paris Beaumont was, in the course of a brief season (May–June 1924), the organizer of truly astonishing spectacles that must be counted among the most stimulating of their time. Although irritating to the lovers of traditional ballet, the creations of Les Soirées de Paris consisted of both danced pantomime and tableaux vivants, whether the individual work was Cocteau and Jean Hugo's *Roméo et Juliette* or *Mercure* ("plastic poses" in three scenes) by Massine, Satie, and Picasso.

The eroticism of *Mercure* and Picasso's "found objects" provoked vigorous protests from the public. But Diaghilev—even though uninvited and disturbed by Beaumont's undertaking, which he saw as a possible threat to himself—attended that evening and loudly expressed his enthusiasm.

It was in 1924 as well that Gabrielle Chanel engaged Étienne de Beaumont as director of design for her new line of jewelry.

△ Beaumont, as much as his wife, had fascinated Radiguet, who made this very Parisian couple the main characters in his novel *Le Bal du comte d'Orgel*, which appeared in 1923.

△◁ The Comte de Beaumont's love of charades and tableaux vivants became the fashion. Every party in Paris served as an occasion for spectacle. Here, at the home of Prince Jean-Louis de Faucigny-Lucinge, are the actor and producer Marcel Herrand with Comtesse de Beaumont and Chanel, done up as a fakir!

▷ The Comte de Beaumont, as portrayed by Pablo Picasso.

Chanel

Chanel in her Russian period

Biarritz thronged with émigrés

Tsarist Russia had utterly collapsed. Biarritz, meanwhile, was the rendezvous for those Russians who, after escaping the massacre, found refuge in France. Here Marthe Davelli, the beautiful opera singer, introduced her friend Chanel to Grand Duke Dimitri Pavlovitch. Twenty-one years old, he was a bachelor and a very handsome man. His presence on the historic night in January 1917 when the monk Rasputin was assassinated had endowed him with a certain mystery. It made him seem a Lorenzaccio, like Alfred de Musset's hero, which he was not.

△ Chanel in 1920 at Biarritz during her brief liaison with Grand Duke Dimitri, who was eleven years her junior. They became inseparable for a year and remained loyal friends thereafter.

▷ Grand Duke Dimitri in 1914 as a Lieutenant in the Guards Regiment.

Slavic charm

"Princes of the blood have always filled me with immense pity. Their métier, when they practice it, is the saddest thing possible, and still sadder when they don't practice it," Chanel said to Morand in 1919. And Dimitri, it is true, had experienced an extremely sad childhood. His mother, Alexandra of Greece, died just after he was born. Then his father, Grand Duke Paul, married a divorcée, which caused him to be banished by his cousin the Tsar and thus separated from his two children. At age eleven, Dimitri and his sister were placed with their Uncle Sergei, the governor of Moscow, and his wife, the Tsaritsa's deeply religious sister. In reality, Grand Duke Dimitri was brought up by nurses.

Chanel was quicker than anyone to understand Dimitri's singular form of misery, which was to grow up without a mother. But what fascinated her about this Prince was his innate sense of luxury. She succumbed to Slavic charm.

▽ January 21, 1924. Lenin dies and Stalin becomes his successor. Now, revolution shows its true face to Russian émigrés: not a passing cataclysm but an irreversible situation. And then a wave of assistants arrives in the Chanel salon, mostly ruined and uprooted aristocrats. They become salesladies or models, and speak Russian among themselves. At lunch time they all meet at Aux Fleurs, a tea room on the Faubourg Saint-Honoré.

1920–1923: the Dimitri years

A great event in the career of Chanel occurred in 1920 when she launched No. 5, presented in a spare, minimal bottle—a flagon as clean as a cube—that stood in stark contrast to the frippery then favored by perfumers. No. 5 was a mixture of 128 ingredients, blended by an eminent chemist, Ernest Beaux, whose father had been employed at the tsarist court.

It is difficult to invoke luck as the only cause of the meeting between Gabrielle Chanel and Ernest Beaux in Grasse, in the laboratory where No. 5 was born. Or luck that this perfume technician had been the son of a court employee of the tsars. Or that he spent his youth in St. Petersburg. Unless we give luck another name: Dimitri Pavlovitch, Chanel's friend and lover.

▷ Ernest Beaux, who produced the first Chanel No. 5 perfume: the building block of Gabrielle's immense fortune. Beaux proposed five different formulas and she chose the last.

page 186: In 1920 Chanel made a timid use of embroidery, which *Vogue* applauded.

page 187: Sem celebrates Chanel No. 5, a key source of Coco's fortune.

Rendezvous at Garches, 1920–23

△ In the early 1920s Chanel invited Grand Duke Dimitri and his valet, Piotr, to Garches, where she had acquired a villa. The playwright Henri Bernstein, who first captivated the *boulevard* public in 1903, was her neighbor and also one of her numerous admirers. Here Chanel, clad in a "sports cape," takes the Bernsteins' little daughter for a stroll in Garches. Beginning in this period, Chanel was regarded as the creator of "sports" fashion in France, and the press coverage she received grew more serious every day.

◁△ The cape of the American YMCA volunteers prompted Chanel to create the "sports" cape that she featured in her 1920 collection and wore in the streets of Garches.

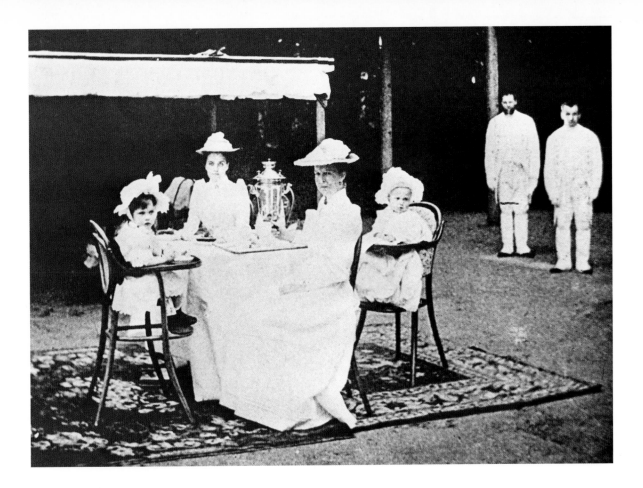

△ 1894: Tea in the garden at Ilinskoie, the home of Grand Duke Sergei. Dimitri and his sister, under the supervision of nanny Fry and the assistant nurse, Miss Grove. One of the valets, Piotr, followed Dimitri into exile and lived with him at Chanel's home in Garches.

◁ Sketch of a Chanel creation in *Vogue*, 1922. A blouse in kasha-colored khaki, with a skirt buttoned on the side. The sole ornament, a brown leather belt. Obviously, Russia had entered the designer's life.

◁◁ Grand Duke Dimitri of Russia spent his childhood putting on a succession of marvelous military uniforms. Here, at age eleven, he wears the eagle-crowned helmet of the Imperial Guard.

CHEZ CHANEL
LA PARISIENNE DE BON GOUT EST DANS SON ÉLÉMENT

*Tout ce qui, à Paris, s'intéresse à l'élégance, passe
dans les salons de Chanel, et c'est un plaisir pour
les yeux que ces réunions de jeunes femmes dont
la toilette est étudiée jusqu'au moindre détail. Trois
mannequins ondulent au milieu du salon : celui
de gauche montre un manteau en lamé rose et
argent garni de chinchilla imitation. Au centre
est un costume en laine tricotée et kasha beige. La robe
à trois volants est en Georgette noir, avec petite cape*

Olga Thomas, drawing in *Vogue*, November 1920. Chanel tunic and skirt ensemble embroidered with the chain stitching typical of her Russian period. The embroidered dresses proved so popular that Chanel created a workshop dedicated entirely to embroidery. The *directrice* was Grand Duchess Marie, Dimitri's sister.

An embroidered coat by Chanel. *Vogue*, 1922.

Here, with square décolletage, the Russian tunic (*rubachka*) is made of black crêpe de chine. Drawing by Reinaldo Luza in *Vogue*, 1922.

Sketch in *Vogue*, 1923. At Deauville there was a show of Chanel furs modeled by Russian ladies, who wore them with such ease that the rich garments seemed like everyday clothes. Whenever the mannequins encountered Dimitri, they called him "Your Majesty" and kissed his hand, to the great astonishment of the French public.

1923–1924: a Russian collection

Imagine a more singular liaison than that of Gabrielle Chanel with the Grand Duke Dimitri Pavlovitch. She, the daughter of a fairgrounds peddler who, somewhere in France, was still hawking suspenders and handkerchiefs from his pushcart at "2 francs a dozen"; he, the grandson of Alexander II, nephew of Alexander III, cousin of the last Tsar, who treated him as his own son, probably because the Tsarevitch had such precarious health.

Chanel adopted the Russian peasant blouse—the long, belted *rubachka* traditionally worn by *muzhiks*—and made it the uniform of chic Parisiennes. Clearly, Russia had entered the designer's life.

◁ Woodruff, drawing in *Vogue*, 1923. Never would so many fur coats and fur linings be seen at Chanel's as in these years.

Picasso, Diaghilev, Cocteau:
the prodigious decade

Montparnasse replaces Montmartre

If Cubism was born in Montmartre, it was in Montparnasse that the style matured and became a kind of lingua franca of modern art and design. Nothing could have been more different from the Montmartre bohemia than the culture that replaced it. But in 1920 no actual break occurred between these two cradles; far from it. What could not be tolerated, as Jean Cocteau would remark, was going off the chosen route: "The Cubist code prohibited every journey except the north-south one, between the Place des Abessess and the Boulevard Raspail." Actually, it was in the period immediately before World War I that this shift took effect, as Guillaume Apollinaire noted in *Paris-Journal*, where he announced that "the daubers no longer feel at home in modern Montmartre, now full of phony artists, commercial fantasists, and happy opium-smokers. The real artists, meanwhile, are to be found in Montparnasse, all dressed like Americans."

△ Left to right: Oritz de Zarate, the Chilean painter whom Apollinaire called "the only Patagonian in Paris," and who stood by Modigliani in his last days; Max Jacob, the Breton Jew who the year before had been baptized with Picasso as his godfather; Moïse Kisling the Pole, an incorrigible reveler; and Picasso the Spaniard, whose cap permits us to place the photo in time as precisely as if Picasso had dated it himself: 1917, the wartime year of *Parade*. The sole woman in the group is Pacquette, a conquest of Picasso's and one of those ineluctable figures always to be found in cafés where artists hang out. Location: La Rotonde. The photographer: Jean Cocteau.

And in the life of Picasso . . .

. . . We move from bohemia to bourgeois comfort. Olga Khoklova, Russian lady, daughter of an army officer, balle-rina of modest rank in the Diaghilev company, replaced the beautiful Fernande, artisan's daughter and Picasso's model and mistress in the Bateau-Lavoir days. Fernande had been part of the great adventure, with its difficult beginnings among joyous bohemians. Olga, whom Picasso wed on July 12, 1918, meant family life in a vast middle-class apartment on the Rue La Boétie, during that brief and curious period when Picasso was breaking away from Montmartre and moving into swank neighborhoods.

About the wedding, Cocteau, Picasso's witness at the Russian Orthodox ceremony, wrote to his mother: "I held a golden crown over the head of Olga, and we all looked as if we were playing *Boris Godunov*. A beautiful ritual. A real wedding. Lunch at the Meurice. Misia in sky blue. Olga in white *satin-tricottulle*. Very Biarritz."

△ Picasso and the beautiful Fernande Olivier in the days of the Bateau-Lavoir in Montmartre, about 1908.

◁ Picasso and Olga Khoklova in London, one year after their marriage. They were the toast of the "gentry." By this time the artist had begun to wear clothing of a sort never seen on him before. Even as his friends raised their eyebrows, he added a gold watch and chain to his vest. Juan Gris, disgusted, wrote to Kahnweiler: "Picasso still does beautiful things, when he has the time . . . ! Between a Russian ballet and a fashionable portrait."

Photos Wladimir Rehbinde

"Chanel goes Greek"

This headline contains an element of surprise, since it did not concern fashion and appeared on the theatre page. Chanel was collaborating with artists who ten years later would make the informed public come running, but who at this time—1923—had yet to make their mark.

Antigone, in a free adaptation by Cocteau, with sets by Picasso, music by Honegger, and costumes by Chanel— this was the announcement posted at the Atelier, the theatre that Charles Dullin had just taken over and would direct for the next twenty years. Dullin and Chanel had known one another since about 1916, when he shared life with Caryathis high up on Montmartre in the studio where Chanel took her classes in eurythmic dance. Because of this old friendship, one can surmise that it was as much thanks to the demanding director of the Atelier as to Cocteau himself that Chanel received her first opportunity in the theatre.

This *Antigone*, in the opinion of some, would prove to be little more than a fatuous distraction for a few aesthetes, since those responsible for the production had

△ Drawings by Georges Lapape commissioned for the French edition of *Vogue* as illustrations for an article devoted to Cocteau's *Antigone*. The piece appeared in February 1923.

limited or nonexistent knowledge of the classical theatre. Chanel, for instance, had never done a theatrical costume in her life. As for Picasso, not to mention Cocteau, what could he make of Sophocles, having until then designed sets for nothing but the *bouffonneries* that the Comte de Beaumont, a sort of master of "society in revolt," made his specialty.

With Cocteau, Picasso, and Chanel

Rave notices in the foreign press, whose opinion found no or almost no counterpart in Paris. The new style of *Antigone* baffled the critics, despite the clarification that Cocteau fed to the journalists: "The characters in *Antigone* do not explain themselves. They act. They represent the kind of theatre that must replace the theatre of chit-chat." But it was the theatre of chit-chat produced by the likes of Sacha Guitry that the Parisian public liked. And the Cocteau production—with its antique masks

clustered about a loudspeaker serving as a choir, its actresses made up in white, its actors made up in red, and Antonin Artaud (who played Tiresias and in real life was Atanasiou's lover) reaching paroxysms of fury in his imprecations—left audiences dumbfounded. The press compared Picasso's masks grouped about a loudspeaker, and the black shields with motifs taken from Delphi, to store windows during Mardi Gras.

△ Antigone between her two guards. Only Chanel's costumes found favor: "These woolen clothes in neutral tones look like antique garments rediscovered after centuries," observed *Vogue*. Meanwhile, Cocteau declared: "I ordered costumes from Chanel because she is the greatest couturière of our time."

△ A Greek actress, Genica Atanasiou, was an Antigone with close-cropped hair, plucked eyebrows, and eyes outlined in black and drawn toward the temples. Chanel's costume for Antigone was a long cape of patterned brown wool.

△◁ Belted about Dullin's head is a rather barbaric-looking band, probably the first piece of jewelry to come from the hands of Gabrielle Chanel.

◁ Chanel's costumes for Hemon and Creon. Dullin, according to Cocteau, played Creon as a tyrant "drunk with rage and stupid power."

This headline, which ran in a 1923 issue of *Harper's Bazaar*, marked a turning point in Chanel's career, for the recognition of Baron de Meyer, who wrote the article, counted for more than mere publicity: it amounted to a consecration. This was true, first of all, because of the Baron's exalted social standing. Of German nationality, he was simply Demeyer Watson before gaining a title by virtue of his marriage to a natural daughter of Edward VII. Or perhaps it was Kaiser Wilhelm II; There was always a doubt. Cecil Beaton, who admired him enormously, called him "the Debussy of the camera." De Meyer had become a peerless photographer. The grace and Whistlerian style of his portraits would never be surpassed.

1920–1924: The Chanel style turns its back on the past

In the years 1920–24 Chanel became an international figure, a magnetic individual sought after and invited everywhere. Such universal welcome constituted a significant departure in the annals of society, for "1900 did not receive its *fournisseurs*, even if they were Monsieur Doucet and Madame Lanvin," as Paul Morand correctly noted in his book on Chanel. About this brief period in society, Chanel could say with pride: "I did not go into society because I had to design clothes. I designed clothes precisely because I did go out, because I was the first to live the life of this century. . . . Fashion is not simply a matter of clothes; fashion is in the air, borne upon the wind; one intuits it; it is in the sky and on the macadam; it comes from ideas, manners, events. . . . If, for example, there are no more *robes d'intérieur*—those tea gowns so dear to the heroines of Bourget and Bataille—it is undoubtedly because we live in an age when there aren't any more interiors." And indeed it

△ The engaging Baron Gayne de Meyer. Photograph by George Hoyningen-Huene.

▷ As an illustration for the de Meyer article, Drian made this drawing of Gabrielle Chanel.

was not only fashions that changed in these years. Textiles, colors, architecture, furniture—everything was in the process of changing. It was all moving toward the explosion of 1925, for the world itself was undergoing change. But had one told Gabrielle that she was hitting her stride at a historic moment, would she have understood? Whole pieces of the past were simply crumbling away. How could Chanel have known, she who, as it happened, had no past? This was her tremendous advantage. No woman could have been less concerned about her social success. "Society" had never before opened its doors to couturières, however talented they may have been, and these creative women had been relegated to the status of *faiseuses* or "dressmakers" (with the word couturier used only in the masculine). Then, suddenly, for Chanel everything changed. But it all seemed perfectly natural to her, as natural as the revolution in style that she helped to bring about.

△ Drawing of a Chanel dress published in *Vogue*, 1924. Now young women could scandalize their mothers with a new set of gestures, such as applying their lipstick in public.

VICTOR MARGUERITTE

La garçonne

E. FLAMMARION, EDITEUR

1920–1925: Emancipated women and innovators

◁ *La Garçonne* appeared in July 1922 and quickly became the novel people were snatching out of one another's hands. It created a scandal, causing the author to be stricken from the rolls of the Legion of Honor.

▽◁ Chanel invented beach pajamas, here seen in their first version. A woman in pants! The sight created panic in Garches.

▽ At Garches, Henri Bernstein donned pajamas like those worn by Chanel—unisex before its time!

△◁ "Many women in bathing suits have a masculine and somewhat singular appearance. They look like boys who have just taken their baccalauréat." Drawing by Berings, *L'Illustration*, 1925.

△ At La Potinière in Deauville women began to smoke like men. Drawing by Berings, *L'Illustration*, August 1925.

◁ Stravinsky opted for French citizenship. He left Switzerland in 1920 and, accompanied by his family, moved in with Chanel, remaining there about two years. In 1922 the composer sent this photo to Diaghilev, inscribed: "I send you this questionable copy of a good photo of my mug, a family-type photo." Stravinsky was very smitten with Chanel, who all her life would cherish the icon that he gave her on his arrival in her home, where, under commission from Diaghilev, he orchestrated the themes for the ballet *Pulcinella*.

GRANDE SAISON D'ART DE LA VIIIᵉ OLYMPIADE

BALLETS RUSSES
DE
SERGE DE DIAGHILEW

THÉATRE DES CHAMPS-ÉLYSÉES
MAI-JUIN 1924

III.

LE TRAIN BLEU

CREATION

Opérette dansée en un acte

Scénario de Jean COCTEAU
Musique de Darius MILHAUD
Chorégraphie de LA NIJINSKA
Costumes de CHANEL
Décors de H. LAURENS

La scène se passe sur une plage en 1924.

LA CHAMPIONNE DE TENNIS	Mᵐᵉˢ NIJINSKA
PERLOUSE	Lydia SOKOLOVA
BEAU GOSSE	MM. Antoine DOLINE
LE JOUEUR DE GOLF	Léon WOIZIKOVSKY

LES POULES :	LES GIGOLOS :
Mᵐᵉˢ CHOLLAR, DEVALOIS, DOUBROVSKA, ALLANOVA, MAIKERSKA, NIKITINA I, CHAMIE, SOUMAROKOVA I, ZALEVSKA, COXON, KOMAROVA, KRASOVSKA, NIKITINA II, SOUMAROKOVA II, ROSENSTEIN, NEMTCHINOVA.	MM. ZVEREW, SLAVINSKY, SLAVINSKY, FEDOROW, PAVLOW, TCHERKAS, LIFAR, LAPITSKY, SAVITSKY, NIKITINE, SINGAEVSKY, KOCHANOVSKY, MICHAILOW, HOYER.

Orchestre sous la direction de M. André MESSAGER

Diaghilev takes the "Blue Train"

In January 1924 Sergei Diaghilev found himself so seduced by the music of Christiné and Yvain and the popular forms of French operetta that he began to think of commissioning a scenario in that spirit. Deliver ballet from its mists and veils and give it a touch of reality—who could better effect such a renewal than Jean Cocteau? With *Le Boeuf sur le toit* and then with *Les Mariés de la tour Eiffel*, he had already shown the way. Thus it was to Cocteau that Diaghilev took his idea. *Le Train bleu*, a ballet combining acrobatics, satire of the period, and pantomime, came forth as a "danced operetta."

△ Darius Mihaud with Sergei Diaghilev, whom Igor Markevitch characterized as a "prodigious *agent provocateur*," a quality he shared with Jean Cocteau.

For his "Blue Train" music, Diaghilev went to Darius Milhaud, who found the request most unusual: "I had never thought of writing an operetta . . . even without words. I accepted the challenge."

In the spring of 1924 Diaghilev visited Picasso and found himself stopped in his tracks by a painting of two monumental, tunic-clad women whose shoulder straps have fallen away to reveal the figures' breasts. As they race along the beach, the women seem ecstatic with sand, sea, and wind—the very image of joyous running. Right off, Diaghilev wanted to make the painting into the forecurtain for *Le Train bleu*. Picasso felt uncertain about the idea, but no one could resist Diaghilev, and so, while unenthusiastic, the artist gave in.

Diaghilev assigned the execution of the curtain to one of his closest collaborators, Prince Schervachidzé, a Georgian émigré whose talent in such matters bordered on the prodigious. His role in comtemporary ballet decoration was a crucial one, since he transposed painted sketches so faithfully that he reproduced minor errors and accidents.

△ The forecurtain for *Le Train bleu*, executed by Prince A. Schervachidzé, after a painting by Picasso. As a salute to the picture, Diaghilev commissioned Georges Auric to compose a fanfare.

When opening night came and Picasso saw the curtain for the first time, he was so impressed with the work of the prince-artisan that immediately, at the bottom of a work he had never touched, the master wrote: "Dedicated to Diaghilev." After which, without the slightest hesitation, he signed: "Picasso. 24."

To give choreographic expression to a scenario bringing together bathers, tennis players, golf champions, and beautiful young things in search of adventure, Diaghilev chose Bronislava Nijinska, who was as stubborn as her illustrious brother. She spoke not a word of French and, moreover, knew nothing about the famous Blue Train to the south of France. Separated from the Ballets Russes throughout the war, detained in Russia, and deeply marked by the Revolution, she had no taste for either luxury or laughter.

▷ In 1923, after taking charge of the Ballets Russes programs, Boris Kochno tried in vain to get Picasso's permission to reproduce the studies the artist had made of the company dancers during their season in Rome in 1917. Alas, the sketches could not be found in the disorder of Picasso's studio. Then, just as Kochno was about to leave, "Picasso, as if seized by a sudden inspiration, took a pencil from his pocket and, in a matter of minutes, covered the maquette, page by page, with the most wonderful drawings." Reproduced here, these drawings appeared in the *Train bleu* program, making it a sumptuous publication indeed.

Cocteau suggested that Nijinska seek inspiration in photographs of Suzanne Lenglen playing tennis and of the Prince of Wales on the golf course. Both failed to move her. Diaghilev himself served as interpreter and mediator, but right away Cocteau and Nijinska began to detest each other. She reserved for herself the role of the Tennis Player. Small and heavily muscled, she was, like Nijinsky, rather short of leg, and with her fleshy mouth and almond eyes, she very much resembled her brother. She also had his strength and was equally opinionated. Diaghilev thought her the greatest choreographer of her time: "Whatever one may think, that extravagant little lady . . . comes from the Nijinsky family, which says everything."

Premiered in June 1924 at the Théâtre des Champs-Elysées, *Le Train bleu* formed part of "the season of art at the 8th Olympiad," in which Diaghilev's Ballets Russes proved to be the main event.

◁ The role of Beau Gosse went to a young English dancer, Anton Dolin, who had been trained in the Russian school of Princess Astafieva, formerly a dancer at the Maryinsky Theatre in St. Petersburg. With his hair slicked down and parted in the center, Dolin was a marvel, completely athletic and the very image of a beachcombing Don Juan of the 1920s.

▷ Opening night for *Le Train bleu*. From left to right: Perlouse, danced by Sokolova (Hilda Munnings from England and, in 1913, the first non-Russian *première danseuse* ever engaged by Diaghilev); Beau Gosse, in the person of Dolin; Cocteau, the scenarist; Golf Player, a role taken by Leon Woizikovski, brought from Poland in 1915; and the Tennis Player, the part that Nijinska reserved for herself.

Suzanne Lenglen, who at age fifteen had become tennis champion of France, delighting the British with her sensational leaps, served as the model for Cocteau's Tennis Player in *Le Train bleu*. The tennis vogue in France was due mainly to Lenglen, the invincible queen of Wimbledon in singles as well as doubles from 1919 to 1924. The way Lenglen had of dressing contributed to her legend. No woman champion before her had ever worn two cardigans, one on top of the other, nor a strip of fabric wound about the head like a bandage. Chanel used this in the headdress she designed for Nijinska.

Baron de Coubertin, president of the Olympic Committee, and the members of his committee, all present and cited, filled the hall and two pages of the program. As Armand Lanoux has noted in his study of the years around 1925: "The only revolution, basically, is sport. 1900 had the velocipede, horses, the first racing cars; 1925 brought athleticism, boxing, the stadium. . . ."

Sets by a sculptor: Henri Laurens

It was not a painter but a sculptor who did the set for *Le Train bleu*. A Cubist, Henri Laurens had never in his life prepared a stage design. But it was this most Parisian of Parisians that Diaghilev asked to re-create a fashionable beach scene, this son of a laborer who took on the task of transposing to the theatre the frivolity of a summer holiday. Laurens, like Milhaud, liked a challenge. And he han-

dled the Côte d'Azur *cabines* in a strange way, making them look striped and truncated. When finished, the set resembled a collage. It completely changed the sense the audience had of the elegant beaches where each day the Blue Train discharged its cargo of bathers.

◁ Henri Laurens—the taciturn artist whose friends included Braque, Gris, Picasso, and Modigliani (the author of a magnificent portrait of a bearded and long-haired Laurens)—had remained unknown to the world of evening galas. The exceptions in this crowd, however, were two famous collectors who happened to be at the *Train bleu* premiere: Jacques Doucet and Charles de Noailles (the one owned a "fountain" and the other a "fireplace" by Laurens). The artist had also been known to Raymond Radiguet, whose *Pélicans* he had just finished illustrating. Fame arrived late for Laurens. Only after World War II did he receive the attention he merited. Ironically, the proud sculptor had long said: "We are all the products of our time and social environment—that is, if we are not plagiarists of the past."

Costumes bearing the signature of Chanel

For the *Train bleu* costumes, Diaghilev went to Chanel, who worked to the very letter of the assignment as given by Cocteau: "Instead of trying to remain this side of the ridiculous in life, to come to terms with it, I would push beyond. What am I looking for? To be truer than true." Thus, *Le Train bleu* was not danced in costumes that mixed the real with the imaginary but in actual sports clothes, which included beach sandals and golf shoes. Chanel made no attempt to prettify, but instead adorned the dancers with the charm of reality.

△ Chanel during the rehearsals for *Le Train bleu*. She brought to the stage a style that was her own.

△◁ Dolin as Beau Gosse and Leon Woizikowski in the role of the Golfer.

◁ Wearing her swimsuit, Lydia Sokolova in the role of Perlouse, with Leon Woizikowski.

Black magic

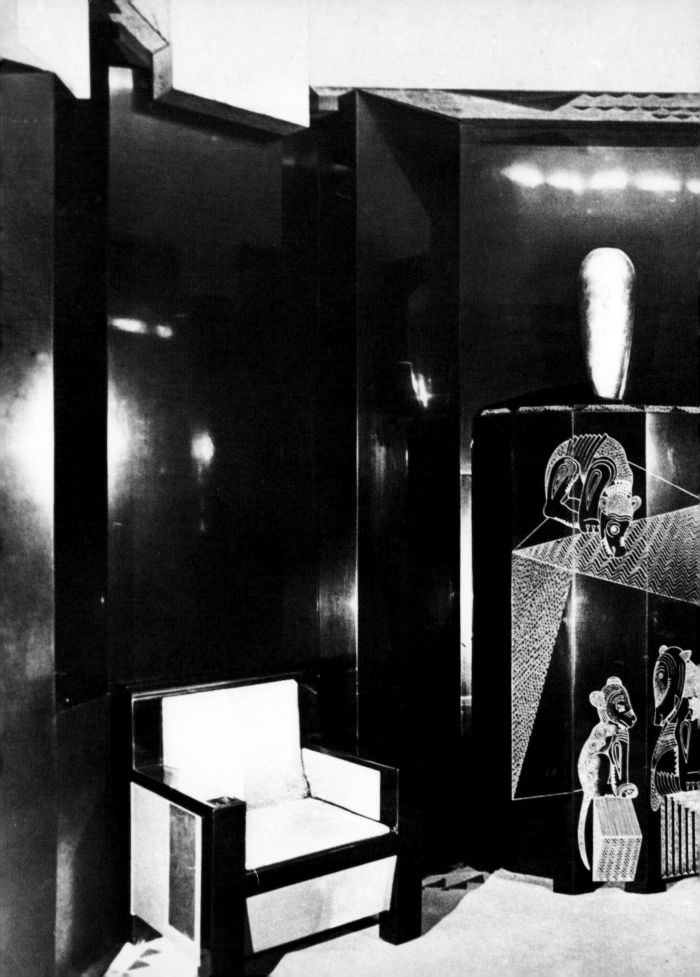

A new term: Art Deco

At the 1925 Exposition des Arts Décoratifs, Jean Dunand completely covered the walls of the "smoking room" in the French pavilion with a glossy black lacquer. Bordering on the Esplanade of the Invalides, the pavilion reflected the sensibilities of France's most respected architects and decorators. With its Baudelairean sumptuousness, with its radiant ceiling illuminating the wall panels, with its shutters of red and silver lacquer, the smoking room would have a decisive influence on world taste in the period before World War II.

1925: the expo of the century

All Paris deplored the fact that the French had allowed Italy to be the first—in 1902 at Turin, in 1906 at Milan, and in 1911 at Rome—to act on an idea that had actually originated in France: the organization of a grand encounter, a sort of competition played out by the best in Europe in the form of an exhibition of modern decorative arts. Artists, industrialists, and craftsmen would join together to display architecture with works in wood, metal, glass, paper, fabric, and ceramic. These might consitute "either utilitarian or purely sumptuary objects in their purpose: public or private buildings, interior and exterior decoration, furnishings, personal adornment. . . ," to quote from one of the reports prepared by the Union Centrale des Arts Décoratifs.

First scheduled for 1915, then pushed forward to 1916, put off by the war until 1922 and 1924, the great event finally opened on April 28, 1925. This manifestation, which Le Corbusier characterized as "an international

△ At the Expo des Arts Décoratifs there was an amusement park along the Seine embankment, which drew few children but crowds of adults. *L'Illustration* characterized it as "an island of joy and exuberance." Among the games was the one illustrated here, called "Negro in the Water." Anyone who threw at the target and hit it would plunge an athletic black man seated on a board into a tank of water. On cold evenings the poor plunger shivered and shook. *L'Illustration*, which published this drawing, wrote: "There is a society for the protection of animals but none yet for Negroes."

marathon of the household arts," would launch a new term: Art Deco. It defined the style of an entire decade. The occasion itself gave birth to a fashion—the love of black—and generated a veritable rage for an intense orange called "the tango color," which together displaced the earlier harmonies, affecting homes and women of every level.

La vogue nègre

It burst upon the scene in 1925, transforming all aspects of daily life. Decorators and ceramists, jewelers and cabinet-makers, silversmiths and bookbinders, silk weavers, poster makers, and glassblowers all "went black." Even the Siegel mannequins created by Vigneau for department-store windows were lacquered black. They had what may have been the desired effect, which was to provoke indignant protest.

221

AMÉRIQUE AFRIQUE

MAGIE NOIRE

PAUL MORAND

Black art had been known since 1905, but only to a very small number of artists and collectors. Suddenly in 1925 it caught the interest of the popular press, thanks mainly to a pair of great successes. First came American jazz, with all its freshness and originality. This brought socialites to the *bals nègres* where they danced the Black Bottom. Fierce competition developed among the boîtes—mainly the Bal Nègre and the Boulle Noire—where Parisians could dance with blacks. All this helped to prepare for the triumph of the *Revue nègre*, which introduced Josephine Baker and Sydney Bechet in secondary roles. With its explosive force, the *Revue nègre* repeated the adventure of the Ballets Russes, revealing to the Paris of 1926 an exotic art of bewitching authenticity.

Paul Morand, monarch of the twenties

The legend of Paul Morand, like that of Chanel, is integral to the mid-twenties. The style and tone of Chanel, her art of living, all find their echo in Morand's style, tone, and writing. These two lived in harmony with their time, Chanel by dressing it and Morand by describing Europe between the wars, already submerged in a mad wave of jazz.

△ *Magie noire* (*Black Magic*) tells of the irresistible and disquieting attraction that the civilized world felt for the black world, a phenomenon that Paul Morand believed to have begun in 1920: "In the bars of the post-Armistice period, jazz produced such sublime and heartbreaking accents that we all understood that we must have a new form of expressing our own feelings. Sooner or later, I said to myself, we must respond to this call from the dark, must go and see what was behind that imperious melancholy coming out of the saxophones."

◁ Here is one of the monarchs of the twenties, dressed in a diving suit. Paul Morand was the greatest sportsman among the writers of his time. Nothing could stop him, and he traveled constantly, from New York to Timbuktu. His philosophy: "The real snobs are in sweaters." Here he simultaneously gave the best definition of the twenties' reverse snobbism and the briefest possible explanation for the success of his friend Coco Chanel. He cultivated a black humor: "After *Black Magic*, even photos of me began—oh, Dorian Gray!—to look negroid."

Paris goes gaga over a naked dancer

When Josephine Baker made her Paris debut in the chorus of *La Revue nègre*, she was only nineteen and completely unknown. Born in St. Louis, she had sung since the age of eight in the nightclubs of Harlem. In Paris she appeared on stage in the nude and created a sensation. Her beautiful black-idol body, her ravishingly lovely bust, her delicate arms and long legs combined with her agility and exotically charming voice to assure the American performer an instantaneous success. Nothing in the history of French theatre could compare with it. Whereas the Ballets Russes drew an elite class, the *Revue nègre* had immense popular appeal, and it made a star of Josephine overnight. This was the order that Chanel, more than anyone else in Paris, understood how to capture and exploit. She too was thirsting for authenticity and naturalness. Beginning in 1925, the Chanel style would develop and stand for the entire notion of modernity.

△ In April 1926 the Chanel collection was worn by models whose coiffure strangely recalled that of Josephine Baker. Drawing in the French edition of *Vogue*.

◁ Josephine Baker posed in the nude for Dunand, who made several portraits of her in lacquer and eggshell. Man Ray photographed her, and Horst left this image of the new "rage of Paris." For a while Josephine made her mark in fashion, encouraging the taste for suntan and shaved armpits. In the words of Pierre Mac Orlan: "Baker, even more than la Miss [Mistinguett], shatters our way of seeing and evokes a primitive order."

◁ In 1926 *Vogue* published this drawing along with the following comment: "Here is a Ford signed 'Chanel,'" referring to the mass production of a car. Despite virulent attacks by male journalists, who deplored so many suppressions—"no more bosom, no more stomach, no more rump"—Chanel's "Ford" had the reception anticipated for it. The naysayers could only resort to irony: "Feminine fashion of this moment in the 20th century will be baptized 'lop off everything.'" The counter-cultural success of the now-famous "little black dress" signaled that no longer could men dictate how women should dress. It was with the simplifying taste of Chanel that the female sex would identify.

1926: a veritable frenzy of black

In 1926 the American edition of *Vogue* predicted that a certain black dress created by Chanel—a simple sheath in crêpe de chine, with long, closely fitting sleeves—would become a sort of uniform for all women of taste. But hordes of women wearing the same dress? Such a forecast seemed totally irrational. Then, to show its readers that this immense success might be due to the impersonal simplicity of the dress, the magazine risked a comparison: Would one hesitate to buy an automobile because it could not be distinguished from another vehicle of the same brand? On the contrary, for the similarity constituted a guarantee of quality. *Vogue* concluded: "Here is a Ford signed 'Chanel.'" Thus, fashion too entered the age of standardization, an evolution that has proved irreversible.

△ The Art Deco style proved to be indisputably successful. Never had a call to order been regarded as more imperative. With the new sense of interior décor—stripped of sculpture and all other ornament—fashion would naturally make an alliance, as it did in the *Élégance* pavilion at the 1925 Expo. Here are two Chanel dresses, one in voile and the other in black satin, as they appeared in the Paris *Vogue* of January 1927. These were the dresses that inspired Paul Poiret to utter his famous remark: "What has Chanel invented? De luxe poverty." He went on: "Formerly women were architectural, like the prows of ships, and very beautiful. Now they resemble little undernourished telegraph clerks."

More black, more Chanel, more drawings by Douglas Polland for *Vogue*, and two novelties that generated great excitement: Moroccan crepe and cloche hats, which provoked further irony from the arbiters of past styles: "As for the hats, they are nothing but plain tea strainers in soft felt, into which women plunge their heads by pulling down, with both hands clutching the bottom. . . . Everything disappears, swallowed up by that elastic pocket—hair, forehead, ears, cheeks, all but the nose. They would surely have used shoehorns, had this been suggested." Thus spoke Sem, somewhat bitterly.

The salon of mirrors

In 1928, on the wave of a prodigious success, Chanel installed her business on three floors at 31, rue Cambon, where the house would remain for the rest of the founder's life. Within the infinity produced by reflecting mirrors, total sobriety reigned. This was the vast salon on the *premier étage* where the haute couture collections would be presented. A room conceived and constructed to look as if it had no walls, it created an impression of endless space by virtue of its mirror revetments. Simple basinlike chandeliers gave off a concentrated light, which the mirrors multiplied. Altogether, Chanel's grand salon typifies the transition from the "roaring twenties" to the 1930s.

Business in general sought a décor uniquely suited to its functions, a décor as removed as possible from the pastiches and fake luxury that had prevailed before Expo 25. Chanel was not the only one who opted for a *style moderne*, an interior conforming to the exigencies of her métier, but she was certainly the only woman who understood how to invest her professional environment with the maximum of purity and unity.

Bathers in black on the beach at Deauville

Chic Paris and less chic Paris rubbed shoulders in an assembly that appeared to have lost the conformism of the prewar era. But the bathing suit—worn very tight—was de rigueur.

By 1926 the little skirt had disappeared, as had the thick, heavy jersey that absorbed water like a sponge. In its stead came a fine, woolen, form-defining jersey. Some women went so far as to adopt a silk jersey that sharply modeled the body in a provocative way, especially when worn by bathers with bosoms and hips, as in the instance of an actress who in 1914 appeared on Parisian screens. She was *la femme* personified in the eyes of the young. This was Musidora, wearing her form-fitting black number designed by Poiret, the first vamp of the French movies. But to be chic in the bathing suit that was the craze of Deauville in 1928, a woman had to be devoid of breasts and look like a boy; otherwise, she would seem a relic of the Belle Époque.

△◁ An Italian review, *Numero*, reproduced this drawing by Tofano on its cover.

△▷ The photos seen here and opposite represent a demimondaine named Suzanne Orlandi, who, as we know, figured in the entourage of Gabrielle Chanel at the time the two women lived among the horsey set centered around Étienne Balsan at the Château de Royallieu. That was in 1908. Twenty years later Baron Foy was still the protector of Suzanne Orlandi and still the great love of her life. Orlandi kept, stored away in enormous boxes, an astonishing quantity of snapshots of herself.

Less and less was fashion made for plump ladies, all the while that physical comfort assumed ever greater importance. But the thirst for freedom had its limits. Thus, beach sandals were not yet worn, and only rarely did a woman risk going into the water or on the sand with bare feet. Instead, everyone wore bathing sandals. Colette, however, was one of the avant-garde, which elicited this tribute from Chanel: "I love Colette with her Apostle's feet." One can appreciate her reluctance to allow the weird fashion of wearing high heels with a swim suit.

Shoes worn with swim suits represented a relapse to 1900. Even while liberated from the tyranny of a corset, the female body still submitted to this one last enslavement: shoes designed for parade. It is true, however, that at Deauville, it was not so much on the beach that one had to be seen as on the boardwalk.

The peculiar eroticism of the spectacle that unfolded at Deauville did not escape *Crapouillot*, in which this description could be read: "One sees women poured into silk bathing suits and seated about tables, their powdered faces making a curious contrast to the rest of their bodies, which have been allowed to retain their natural color. It gives one a strange desire for rape. . . ."

In his *Paris 1925* Lanoux notes that, whether reached by the *40 sous route* or by the "pleasure train," Deauville was an extension of the Bois de Boulogne, where "all the young ladies who have their little dog also have their little automobile." He might also have included "their little Kodak." Photography became a passion that grew as the era increased in narcissism. The more they became marginal, the more the demimondaines revealed themselves to be obsessively preoccupied with their own lives and persons. They used the camera in the same way they used the mirror, as an instrument for measuring their charms. Their albums, in which these ignored women came out of the shadows and appeared in full light, both vindicated and reassured them.

Married, at last

Who was this unknown demoiselle Suzanne Orlandi that became Baroness Foy? The daughter of a well-known and richly maintained opera singer, also a poor girl who fell in love with a man socially her superior, who in turn had loved her since she was in her late teens, and for whom she had a passion that would mark her indelibly. This liaison—which would last a great many years—ended in marriage, with the bride almost forty years old, an age when so many déclassées of her sort were nothing more than "unsold inventory," victims certain to have a solitary old age, fearful of each new day. But Suzanne Orlandi got married, an achievement equal to that of Liane de Pougy when she became Princess Ghika. This, however, did not make her any more likely to be *admise* or received. One can only be amazed by the cruelty and class-consciousness on the part of high society in an age said to be permissive, but in actuality mired in fear and snobbery. It was a society that knew how to use distance and indifference as the effective means of annihilating all intruders.

Social ostracism would have taken a different form in England, where, while maintaining distance, one could have expressed enthusiasm for this delicious little spendthrift, for her whimsy, for her love of costume and disguise. No doubt there would have been articles and biographies as in the case of Pepita, the gypsy dancer descended from Andalusian shoemakers, whose liaison with Lord Sackville-West lasted nineteen years. But nothing of the sort happened to *la petite* Orlandi, who died ignored.

◁ Baron and Baroness Foy.

235

Chanel's English period

Tall, blond, solidly built, and dressed in tweed, the Duke of Westminster required that his valet iron his shoelaces, even though His Grace cared little that his soles may have been worn through. He cultivated a style of life that Chanel found immensely instructive. "Elegant: that is, detached," she said, as if reviving the philosophy of Reverdy.

In England every ingenuity was used to satisfy His Grace's least desire. Once, for instance, a station manager blew a whistle and stopped an express train to permit the great lord to board. It must be said, however, that British Rail had little cause to complain, since each year the Duke rented a special train for the purpose of taking himself and his guests to the Grand National at Liverpool.

The love of Bend'or, Duke of Westminster

In the autumn of 1925 it became known that Monte Carlo would be graced by the presence of the Duke of Westminster, whose name the press never mentioned without adding: "the richest man in England." Westminster's divorce from his second wife, after five years of marriage, was creating more comment than the Duke may have wished, since it was he who appeared to be in the wrong—by reason of a nasty bit of adultery. A shocking business and, worse, carried on in a way totally at variance with the public demeanor normally observed by the British establishment, all of which made the Duke unwelcome at court. Now in Monte Carlo, he met Chanel. When she too referred to him as "the richest man in England," Gabrielle hastened to clarify her meaning: "I say this because, first of all, wealth of such magnitude ceases to be vulgar. It is beyond all envy and assumes the proportions of a catastrophe. Moreover, I say it because wealth makes Westminster the last representative of a departed civilization, a paleontological curiosity."

△ Chanel at home. The spectacular flowering of her business gave Gabrielle the means to make her private residence on the ground floor of an aristocratic *hôtel particulier* at 29, Faubourg Saint-Honoré.

◁ During the time of the Duke of Westminster's affair with Gabrielle, Lucien Chanel was a peddler at country fairs in Auvergne, while Alphonse Chanel, seen here, kept a coffee-tobacco bar in Cévennes. His companion—whom he never married—bore him three children. The Chanel brothers became an embarrassment to a sister ready to assume the title of Duchess. If the press got hold of them, the results could prove irritating.

△ Here, Alphonse and his younger brother, Lucien, hawking newspapers.

A Victorian fantasy

Love letters carried from London to Paris by the continuous back and forth of His Grace's couriers; flowers, fruit, and Scotch salmon, fresh out of the water, conveyed by other special couriers, traveling by the then-extravagant means of an airplane, thus was Gabrielle conquered. Once again, she believed that what was being tied could not be untied. She saw a permanent haven in each of the houses to which the Duke took her: Mimizan, his "cottage" in the Landes, his fishing place in Scotland, Saint-Saëns, the ducal château in Normandy. Most of all,

▷ March 1925. Gabrielle Chanel with the Duke of Westminster at the Grand National. Like Chanel, the women of the gentry wore heavy, hand-knit beige stockings.

Gabrielle came to know Eaton Hall, a truly strange house and the Westminster country seat. The immense scale of it all! It had been an ancestor of Bend'or who decided in 1802 to erect a colossal structure bristling with towers. The whole thing proved to be a disastrous undertaking. From 1802 to 1882 entire fortunes had been blithely spent in the vain hope of improving the roof line and the general appearance of Eaton Hall. Bend'or's grandfather had used up £600,000 trying to crown the towers with pointed roofs, to no benefit whatever.

Eaton Hall, a truly strange country house

What surprised Gabrille about Eaton Hall were its lingering ties to the splendor of Victorian times, when the young princes of the royal family honored the Duke of Westminster by inviting themselves to visit. There they all improvised balls and cotillions, the Queen's richest subject having let it be known that he lived in a state of perpetual celebration. In the age of weekends—Gabrielle's time—had anything changed?

There were usually about sixty guests staying at Eaton Hall. Weekends generally started on Thursday evenings in grand English country houses, and lasted until lunch on Monday. A name card was posted on every guest door, not only for identification but also for encouraging the discreet, late night promiscuity that generally went on. With the ball-room always freshly waxed, one could dance merely by summoning the resident band, which would appear in red jackets and polished shoes. On certain occasions dinner was accompanied by music, provided by the house organist or by orchestras brought in at great expense. Chanel got to know, more or less, the battalion of servants commanded by a head butler who enjoyed considerable prestige. By close study of a floor plan, she also became familiar with the immense galleries and salons in whose chainlike sequences she often got lost.

The architecture of this castle, which teemed with curious memories, evoked both the imagery of a cloak-and-dagger novel and the wild poetry of a drama by Victor Hugo. Its owners had the house demolished after World War II.

△ Another view of Eaton Hall, the country house of the Dukes of Westminster, the way Chanel knew it in the 1930s.

243

Purloined English tweeds
and beautiful sweaters

From 1926 to 1931, during her involvement with the Duke of Westminster, Chanel adopted an English style. She took advantage of everything that charmed her, whether at Eaton Hall or on the ducal yachts, and made these discoveries the dominant themes of her collections.

In 1928, while salmon fishing with His Grace, Chanel and another guest—the Englishwoman Vera Bate—confiscated their host's clothing: jackets, sweaters, pants, and even shoes. Such cross-dressing made for a good giggle, at the same time that it also served to introduce Chanel to Scottish tweeds.

Back in Paris, Chanel made fashion out of the black-sleeved waistcoat, its front striped with the ducal colors, that the valets of Eaton Hall wore for their morning

△ Chanel (right) and Marcelle Meyer, the official pianist of Les Six and the Dada soirées, on the *Flying Cloud*, a four-masted schooner, one of two boats belonging to the Duke.

◁ Chanel, with Vera Bate, while salmon fishing in 1928. Vera had been Gabrielle's good angel, for it was she who introduced the couturière to Westminster, and she who helped Chanel find her way into English society. "Vera" was simply a name adopted by Sarah Arkwright when she went to work for Chanel in 1925. Despite a birth certificate that declared her to be the daughter of a mason, her relationship to the British royal family cannot be doubted.

chores. The beret now donned by elegant women, pulled down flush with the eyelids, was that of the sailors on the Westminster yacht, the *Cutty Sark*.

Chanel, however, surprised her friends in London by accompanying her daytime outfits with jewelry of a sort that no lady of English society would have dared to wear except with a ballgown: pearls cascading over the livery waistcoat, and on the beret a great cluster of stones. A breeze of sumptuosity was wafting over the creations of Chanel. But it was a highly controlled richness. Never—at any time in her life—did Gabrielle Chanel imagine that luxury could have any purpose other than to make simplicity appear remarkable.

△ On the *Flying Cloud*. Hardly on board, His Grace grew impatient for heavy weather. This was what made him happy, for the sea was his passion.

▷ Gabrielle Chanel during her English period. On her wrists she wears the famous jewelry just created for her house by her most recent discovery: Fulco di Verdura. Then starting out, the Sicilian Duke would make a career in Paris, London, and New York.

Among the habitués of Eaton Hall: the Prince of Wales set

After having introduced Chanel to Westminster, Vera Bate also presented her to the heir of the British throne.

One day a young man whom the butler had never seen before rang the bell at 29, Faubourg Saint-Honoré. Was this the home of Mademoiselle Chanel? He had an appointment with Vera, he said. Vera was out, but the young man made a fine impression upon the butler. He seemed very proper indeed. After he had spent two hours in the kitchen, carrying on an animated conversation with the chef, Vera finally arrived. When the butler asked whom he should announce, the visitor answered: "The Prince of Wales." Vera rushed to embrace him. He was her friend and perhaps even a bit more than that, and often came to Gabrielle's house.

At the House of Chanel Vera Bate earned her keep, in part, by affording Coco the advantage of her relationships

△ The Prince of Wales steeple-chasing. King George would eventually order him to give up his favorite, but hazardous, sport.

at the English court. She earned it as well just by being the young lady she was, a person everybody wanted to look like—elegant by nature but even more so because attired à la Chanel, inexpensively since she counted among the society mannequins Gabrielle dressed for nothing. The couturière respected Vera, knowing full well that it was to the Englishwoman that she owed her introduction to Bend'or, the Prince of Wales, and even Winston Churchill, to life at Eaton Hall and British high life in general, complete with racing, fox-hunting, and beautiful lady riders, all so reminiscent of the horsey set at Royallieu twenty-five years earlier.

Could Gabrielle have imagined that twelve years later she would be saved by these very friendships, after Winston Churchill, alerted by Bend'or, telephoned in person—it is assumed—to Paris and arranged for Coco to be released from police custody? She had been placed under investigation for her alleged "collaboration" with the Nazis during their occupation of Paris.

△ Summer 1925, on board the battleship *Repulse*. Edward, Prince of Wales, returning to England at the end of one of his interminable tours, journeys that filled him with an increasingly evident boredom. Forty-five different countries received him with acclaim, as much in Africa as in Latin America.

The new lions

Paris witnessed the birth of a new race of dandies, all much admired by women. It was understood that each of these men owned a "Buga" 35B equipped with compressors, that they all lived by the hectic rhythm of this impressive engine, that they practiced the Bugatti religion, which consisted of venerating the great Ettore Bugatti as much as God, of being known to him, of never trusting their precious invention to the ordinary mechanics of Parisian garages, but rather, at the least alarm, of racing off to the factory in Molsheim, which they entered as if into a temple. Of course, everyone could recite by heart the performances of that artist-mechanic, Ettore, on the racetrack. In 1926 Bugatti meant the avant-garde; it meant thoroughbred. Indeed, the Bugatti Owners' Club was the most select society south of the Channel.

△ *Lena Amsel.* Poster by Schnackenberg.

△ Paul Morand at the wheel of his Bugatti. He was preparing an essay entitled *De la vitesse (On Speed)*, which, beginning in 1923, would go through many large printings. Of all the talented men linked with Chanel, Morand was, by far, the one who best understood her.

Along with this went a sense of style marked by an easy grace, a certain élan, a vitality that led to an intoxication with speed and latent self-destruction. Bugatti had his princes (in Paris, Paul Morand and André Derain, among others). The cult also had its dark pages, pieces in an anthology of crashes from which the adept would read during depressed evenings at the bar of La Coupole. Now would be heard about the tragic end of a dancer from Vienna, a beautiful foreigner who had played in *The Woman in the Golden Mask*, an immensely popular film. A seductress and a ravager. Her name? Lena Amsel. Her conquests? Max Ernst, Aragon, Derain. Lena owned a Buga, a decorative accessory and symbol of a new social status, that of the liberated woman.

One day Lena invited a woman friend to "get up some speed" with her on the route to Barbizon. She challenged Derain to a race, Buga against Buga. It ended in disaster. When Lena's automobile turned over in a field, the two women were killed, burned alive. No one could talk of anything else in Montparnasse, where Derain was bitterly attacked. Indeed, the charges made against him turned ugly: He should not have accepted a challenge from a woman, nor should he have trusted a woman at the wheel. The general view was that women "would never learn how."

au théâtre Antoine — directeur
M. Paston —
        Le Vendredi 9 Juillet
                                    1937
    gala dramatique

Macbeth
par Julien Bertheau   Œdipe - Roi
                                par Jean Cocteau

                                              Jean
                                               ☆

        Shakespeare et Sophocle

par : les jeunes comédiens 37.

    décors de Jean Stéphane et de
g. Monin • Costumes de Stéphane - Jean
Cocteau   et : GABRIELLE CHANEL.

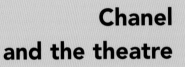

Chanel
and the theatre

◁ Poster of Jean Cocteau
for the "Gala dramatique,"
July 1937.

▷ Chanel in Chanel. Drawing by Jean Cocteau.

Sweaters for *Orpheus*

In 1926 the event of the Paris theatre season was Copeau's surrender of the Théâtre des Arts to Georges and Ludmilla Pitoëff, who forthwith announced a new production: *Orphée*, or *Orpheus*, a one-act tragedy by Jean Cocteau. This brought Chanel, as *Antigone* had, back to the sources of the Greek tragic spirit, for she was to design the costumes. Now the journey would carry her, in the wake of Orpheus, into the kingdom of the dead. Jean Hugo took charge of the sets and made them resolutely contemporary. Pitoëff himself became the director. From Switzerland, Rilke telegraphed his encouragement: "May Jean [Cocteau] feel the warmth of my admiration, he whose poetry alone penetrates into myth, whence he returns tanned as if he had been on the seashore." The production caused a great critical stir, provoking praise and abuse in equal measure.

Orphée marked an important date in the life of Cocteau, for it was now that he took up opium and grew ever-more confident in the magical power of words. It was also during this period that the poet reconciled with Igor Stravinsky.

△ Pitoëff as Eurydice with her sweater-clad Orpheus; behind them, Marcel Herran, who played Heurtebise, a role that Cocteau himself would assume in 1927.

Ties for the Muses

In 1928 Chanel rediscovered her admirer from the days in Garches, Stravinsky, who for a while had made his home in the couturière's villa. During the intervening years Stravinsky had ceased to work with the ballet. The last time he composed for it was in 1920. Now *Apollon musagète* would revive his fruitful collaboration with Diaghilev. Written for strings, this ballet marked Stravinsky's return to classicism. It also joined the artist's name to that of a compatriot whose choreographic inventions were already astounding balletomanes. This was a young Georgian named Georges Balanchivadzé, which Diaghilev abbreviated to Balanchine. Sets and costumes had been assigned to Bauchant, who, however, refused to cooperate with anyone. Without a mock-up of the costumes, Diaghilev improvised, with results that, while satisfactory for Apollo, proved disastrous for the Muses. Called to the rescue, Chanel visualized a free adaptation of the antique tunic, whose pleats she bound with tie silk. Created in 1928 at the Théâtre Sarah Bernhardt, the ballet is now regarded as one of Balanchine's great masterpieces.

△ Felia Doubrovska as a Muse in Balanchine's *Apollon musagète*, with music by Igor Stravinsky and costumes by Chanel.

Death in Venice

The voyage made by the *Flying Cloud* in the summer of 1929 was a strange one. It included the brusque and continuous presence of Misia—in flight from her husband's affair with a much younger woman—at a time when Bend'or and Gabrielle were about to break up. Docking in Venice, Misia and Gabrielle went off in search of Diaghilev. A telegram had alerted Misia that the great impresario was on the Lido, very ill and poorly cared for. His diabetic condition had rapidly deteriorated. Misia and Gabrielle reached him on August 17, 1929, in his room, where, although bedridden, he played the cheerful charmer. But a calm of finality seemed to have come over him. Misia felt certain that he was lost. That evening Diaghilev told Boris Kochno of the pleasure the visit from such loyal friends had given him. He kept repeating: "They were so young, all in white! They were so white."

△ Chanel, whose reputation in Italy was growing, abandoned Deauville for Venice. Here, on the Lido beach, Gabrielle and Misia, two friends "all in white," with Madame Philippe Berthelot in black. Misia had good reason to get away from Paris, where Sert was making her suffer his new and all-too-evident passion, Roussy Mdivani, a Georgian Princess possessed by a longing for self-destruction. An ongoing source of amusement for Parisian society in these years was the spectacle provided by the Sert-Mdivani triangle.

By the night of August 18–19 Diaghilev was dying. Misia ran to his bedside, and was there when in the early morning he breathed his last. As usual, the treasury of the Ballets Russes was empty and actually burdened with a huge deficit. It could not even afford to give Sergei Diaghilev a decent funeral. Chanel stepped in and paid all expenses. In the gray hour of early dawn, a gondola bore the body of this prodigious man to San Michele, Venice's "Island of the Dead." The escort consisted of five friends: Boris Kochno, Serge Lifar, Misia Sert, Catherine d'Erlanger, and Gabrielle Chanel. At the latter's suggestion, the three women took Diaghilev's last words as the expression of a wish. Thus, seated in the black gondola, they were dressed "all in white."

△ In 1929 on the Lido, Gabrielle Chanel launched the first beach pajamas, leaving to her competitors the responsibility for shorts, which she vehemently resisted as an absurd style. For Chanel, only long pants would do, worn with the chic of English officers. Here, a consolidated trio uniformly wearing pajamas: Countess Étienne de Beaumont (wife of the famous Parisian Maecenas and a Chanel client), Gabrielle, and Misia Sert. The two ladies in shorts— Countess Moretti and Signora Chiesa—were the leading hostesses of Venice's *beaux soirs*.

Cocteau/Chanel, a creative friendship

1932–37: These were years in which Chanel's life was much affected by her lively friendship with Jean Cocteau and, on the creative level, by her own growing powers of invention. By now, the couturière's reputation had attained world-wide proportions. And these years, which were so important for Chanel, had their echo in the work of Cocteau, who more and more developed a passion for drawing and an interest in journalism. In 1932 he did the portrait of his collaborator reproduced above, and throughout the period he also produced many drawings of her dress designs, all commissioned for publication in the most prestigious foreign journals. Meanwhile, Cocteau continued to seek Chanel's involvement in his theatrical undertakings.

△ A Chanel dress as interpreted by Jean Cocteau.

△◁ Chanel portrayed by Cocteau, 1932.

▷ Jean Cocteau in 1935 at the time of his *Portraits-Souvenirs* for *Le Figaro*.

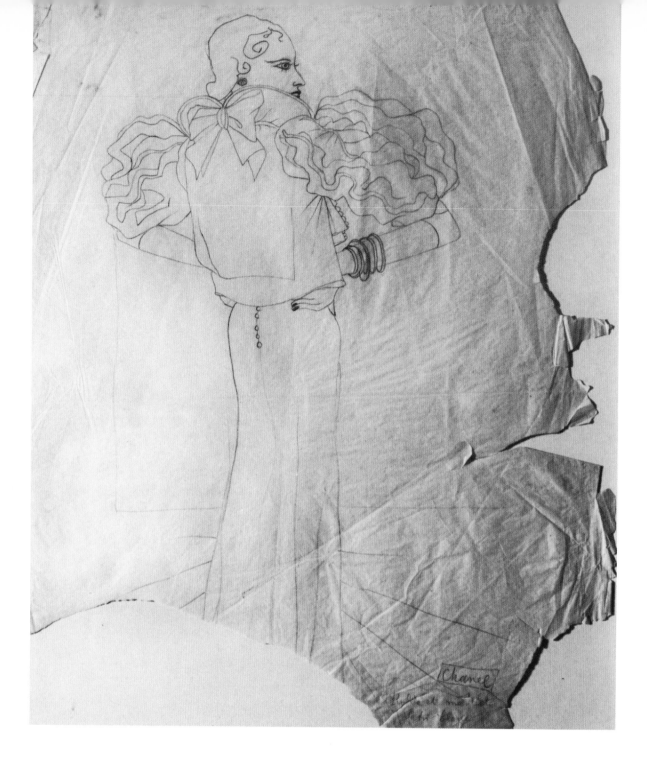

In 1934 Jean Cocteau rediscovered the medieval myth of the Holy Grail and transformed it into a new play for the Théâtre de l'Oeuvre. Presented in 1937, *Knights of the Round Table* unfolded in costumes designed by Gabrielle Chanel.

△▷ A pair of Chanel evening gowns, drawn by Cocteau in the years 1932–35.

robe du soir
de Chanel

Hollywood and the Iribe period

Iribe was the pseudonym taken by Paul Iribarnegaray when, about 1900, he began making satiric drawings. Born in 1883, this native of the Basque country was the exact contemporary of Chanel. By the time of their intimacy, thirty years of cosmopolitan life in Paris still had not erased his indefinable yet distinctive accent. Iribe was only seventeen when *L'Assiette au beurre*, the turn of the century's most famous daily newspaper, began to publish his drawings, and only twenty-three when he established his own paper, *Le Témoin*. No one could sketch an event more tellingly than he.

This was the quality that made Iribe so appealing to the person then known as "Poiret the Magnificent," inspiring the great couturier to have Iribe execute drawings of the models in his collection. From this came an album entitled *Les Robes de Paul Poiret racontées par Paul Iribe*, which, while now valued as a rare, precious book, aroused considerable bitterness within *le beau monde* when the publication first appeared in 1908. "Iribe's album disgusts

△ Paul Iribe in conversation with Cecil B. DeMille in 1923, during the filming of *The Ten Commandments*, for which the Frenchman created the sets.

mothers," wrote Cocteau in his *Portraits-Souvenirs*. Nevertheless, stiffness began to relax and corsets to unlace. As a result, Paul Iribe had a *succès de scandale*. Moreover, commissions started pouring in: furniture for Jacques Doucet, couturier, collector, and bibliophile; fabric of unparalleled richness for Bianchini-Ferrier; jewelled pendants for Lalique. By the 1920s Iribe had become not only the best-known stylist in Paris but also one of the period's great lovers and most newsworthy figures.

Needless to say, the life led by Iribe was a peripatetic one, fueled by success with women, by immense needs for money, and by disputes with clients. The ultimate in luxury, which is always the most ephemeral, was his métier, and no one could have been more fiercely opposed to industrial processes than Paul Iribe. But now weary of it all and ready to give up his creative activity, he began by seducing—and perhaps marrying—a delightful actress, Jane Diris, star of vaudeville, friend of Colette, and pioneer of silent films.

◁ 1924: *Changing Husbands*, a film for which Iribe was director and designer, with Cecil B. DeMille as producer. At the center in an Iribe costume is Leatrice Joy, whose youthful screen debut coincided with the birth of the cinema.

Next Iribe ventured into the world of the wealthy, where each of his liaisons brought him closer and closer to notoriety. Finally, in 1919, he was in Hollywood and married to a rich and beautiful heiress. He also found himself in charge of research for the various films of Cecil B. DeMille, the very man whom Iribe's manifold gifts and accomplishments—drawing, couture, architecture, furniture—or even his weaknesses (the excessive love of luxury, for instance) could not fail to impress.

Changing Husbands

Allowed complete freedom by DeMille, Paul Iribe was simultaneously the director and both set and costume designer for *Changing Husbands*, a film made after his own image. As for developments in Paris, leading toward the great Art Deco exhibition in 1925, he had nothing but contempt, openly expressed. Very much opposed to the

Hollywood saw Iribe as another Poiret, and this was the part he proceeded to play. Like Poiret, Iribe covered furniture in fabrics created for clothing and made clothes from upholstery materials. In him were commingled the couturier and the *meublier*, which can be discerned in a scene from *Changing Husbands*, where one of the protagonists, Varconi, is dressed in a bathrobe made of the same cloth as that in the wall hanging. Now, at first glance, the effect seems comic. Still, it was thanks to Iribe that fashion subsequently strove to become better integrated with the everyday environment.

whole spirit of the event, he denounced "the alliance between Art and the cube." Iribe was for fluid forms, beautiful materials, and a certain profusion. He liked lamés, poufs, fringed cushions, tapestries on the walls, and thick carpets on the floors. According to Iribe, films should, above all else, offer beautiful, entertaining images, and he would undertake to provide them for an eager public.

△ One should also notice the extreme delicacy of the negligée worn by Leatrice Joy. Such transparency struck Hollywood as "very French," meaning "naughty."

In the United States, Iribe benefited from a glamorous reputation. It was he, after all, who had devised the world's most prestigious label, the rose used by Paul Poiret, which was stamped on all the couture tsar's creations with the magic phrase: *Paul Poiret à Paris*. In order to employ an artist of Iribe's caliber, DeMille was prepared to accept everything, expenses as well as caprices. In Hollywood, Paul Iribe enjoyed the status of a star.

◁△ Photographs from *The Ten Commandments*, produced and directed by Cecil B. DeMille, with costumes and sets by Paul Iribe. The latter's Egypt, beautiful but hardly biblical, was an Egypt of the twenties, a place of gilt and lacquer.

Egypt according to Cecil B. DeMille and Paul Iribe

Iribe's power in Hollywood, unlike DeMille's, was not so great that he could be utterly odious without affecting the loyalty and commitment of his team. DeMille was worshipped in the California studios, whereas Iribe made few friends there. Were they all trying to make him pay for his stormy rise? Certainly, Iribe's relations with Mitchell Leisen, one of the best costume designers in Hollywood and, moreover, a faithful member of DeMille's staff, quickly deteriorated into open hostility, plunging the two men

into one of cinema's guerrilla wars. Often the rivalry erupted into strong words, shouting, quarrels, fist fights, and, invariably, the dismissal of one belligerent or the other. In 1923 it was Leisen who lost the battle, which left Iribe alone to create the costumes and sets for a colossal undertaking: *The Ten Commandments*. Produced and directed by DeMille, this film brought the Bible to life. It also had an enormous box-office success.

In 1924 Paul Iribe found himself with a new career opportunity when, with DeMille's blessing, he was given a chance to direct a movie entitled *Changing Husbands*. The results were disastrous. The *New York Times* went so far as to call the film absurd and its direction actually "amateurish." Only Leatrice Joy was spared.

△ A photographic still from *The Ten Commandments*

Right away, DeMille thought it wise to make up with Mitchell Leisen. When the great man put *The King of Kings* into production, he reorganized his staff and restored Leisen as head of the costume department, while leaving the artistic direction to Iribe. Harry Warner would play the leading role: Christ. But a crisis developed in the Golgotha scene, causing DeMille to accuse Iribe of negligence. How was Warner to be held on the Cross? And his hands? How were they going to bleed? None of this had been prepared. DeMille decided to sacrifice someone and right there. Thus, on the summit of this Golgotha it was not Christ who fell victim but Iribe. Sacked! Leisen, on condition that he never again have to work with the Frenchman, agreed to take his place. Iribe left Hollywood without any hope of returning there. But in Paris he was greeted by a present from his American wife: a shop on the Rue du faubourg Saint-Honoré, its facade gleaming with the new owner's name emblazoned upon a lacquer ground. This took Iribe back to his true love: the decorative arts.

△ 1922: Leatrice Joy in *Manslaughter*, a film produced and directed by Cecil B. DeMille. Dressed by Iribe, Joy created such a sensation that the designer received an immediate promotion. He became artistic director.

Iribe and Poiret, interior decorators

1924: *L'Illustration* inaugurated a series of "visits" to Parisian interiors with a piece on "le home exotique et audacieusement moderne" of a performing artist: Mademoiselle Spinelly. A tart and peppery singer, she had been formed in the hard school of café-concert and, like Maurice Chevalier, had made her debut in the streets of Montmartre, playing before an audience of laborers. Around 1901 she was found to have the talent of a *chanteuse gaie*. By 1922 Spinelly had made the cover of *L'Illustration* in a portrait by J.-G. Domergue. But true consecration came in 1924, when Poiret decorated her "studio" and Iribe her bedroom. This Spinelly, if contemporary accounts are to be believed, was a distinctively Parisian personality: "Perched upon an orange divan, drawing about her a multicolored lamé cloak, embroidered, and trimmed in monkey fur, set before a red-lacquer screen, and flanked by white parrots and a crystal basin, Spinelly is almost excessively the woman of today."

△ Domergue, portrait of "Spi."
A prominent star, Spinelly was successful in London and the United States as well as in Paris. Confronted with such an orgy of fashion ideas, one can only repeat Chanel's remark: "Let us beware of originality; in couture it leads to costume, and in theatre to interior design."

△ ◁ A corner of the atrium, created by the atelier of Martine, a firm of considerable fame established by Paul Poiret in 1912. Note the profusion of cushions on the divan. "Too much of everything," said Colette.

△ The dining room done in the English manner, but a manner reinvented by Paul Iribe. The floor made of white marble set with green strips.

◁ The neo-Pompeian atrium, with a floor in gold mosaic and a huge skylight supported by lacquered columns. Decorating the walls are reliefs of trees with gilded leaves. At the center, a mirror-lined pool.

Colette pens a portrait of Chanel at work

Where and when did Colette meet Chanel? Certainly these two knew one another in the twenties, if only through Misia Sert, whose rather close relationship with the great writer is confirmed in the latter's *Journal intermittent*. Between Colette and Chanel, however, feelings were not so friendly. It appears that something other than friendship drew them together—perhaps a sense of revenge upon a past that in some respects was similar for the two women. Before their "success," they both had known not only social opprobrium but also the stern law of necessity. Then too there was their common love of fine craftsmanship, which meant so much to Colette, as can be seen in her portrait of Chanel absorbed in her work, written in 1932 and published in *Prison et Paradis*.

The little black bull as seen by Colette

"If every human face bears a resemblance to some animal—beaked, muzzled, nostriled, trunked, maned—then Mlle Chanel is a little black bull. Is there something of the Camargue here [France's cattle-raising region]? Auvergne asserting its primitive stock. . . . But never mind, for in her butting energy, in her way of facing up to things, of listening, in the defensiveness that sometimes raises a barricade across her face, Chanel is a black bull. That tuft of dark, curly hair, the attribute of bull-calves, falls over her brow all the way to her eyelids and dances with every movement of her head. It is in . . . her work that one must see this reflective conqueror.

"She is said to be very rich. Luckily, she remains uninfected by the contagious glitter of gold, the indiscreet glow exuded by weak souls overwhelmed with possessions.

"There she is, her heels dug into raw materials, between pilasters of jersey, beams of printed foulards, piles of them. Long streams of rolled satin shimmer—a chaos of elastic masonry whose collapse makes not the slightest noise. The very walls of the room swell with mute flannels, downy woolens—all here is silence. A figure, silent except for a ready murmur of acquiescence, holds her breath: Mlle Chanel is engaged in sculpting an angel six feet tall. A golden-blond angel, impersonal, seraphically beautiful, provided one disregards the rudimentary carving, the paucity of flesh, and the cheerlessness—one of those angels who brought the devil to earth.

"The angel—still incomplete—totters occasionally under the two creative, severe, kneading arms that press against it. Chanel works with ten fingers, nails, the edge of the hand, the palms, with pins and scissors right on the garment, which is a white vapor with long pleats, splashed with crushed crystal. Sometimes she falls to her knees before her work and grasps it, not to worship but to punish it again, to tighten over the angel's long legs—to constrain some expansion of tulle. . . . Ardent humility, of a body before its preferred work. With her loins taut and her feet tucked under her thighs, Chanel is like a prostrated laundress beating her linens, like those demanding manageresses who train and entreat day after day, twenty times a day, like the quick genuflections of nuns. This professional involvement of the body leaves her thin and hollow with fatigue. At such a moment I see the nape of her neck, which is devoured by black hair, hair that grows with a vegetal vigor. She talks while working, in a low, deliberately contained voice. She talks, teaching and admonishing, with a sort of exasperated patience. I can make out reiterated words, hummed like basic musical motifs: 'I have a horror of *petits machins*. . . . How many times must I say that fullness is slenderizing? I will not allow myself to say it again . . . . Press down there, ease up here. . . . No, *petits machins* are not needed on a fabric that can speak for itself. . . . Bear down here, release it from there on. . . . No, don't skimp. . . . I won't allow myself to repeat. . . .'

"That meekness, which Chanel exacts—and obtains—from herself surprises me more than her authority, because I have read on her face what is most legible: two long, black, unplucked eyebrows, despotic, apt to come together, raise, and lower—above all, lower! quivering every time they are annoyed by the dancing tuft of hair. . . . From these eyebrows one's attention moves down to the mouth, but there I am not so sure, for in moments of concentration and discontent the middle of the face seems to become concave, sucked in, drawn back under the hood of the eyebrows, under the black volute of hair. It's no more than an instant, but one of total silence, of fierce retreat, a momentary petrification from which the mouth suddenly escapes—the lips flexing, corners turned down, impatient, tamed, punished by cutting teeth.

"The angel-mannequin has left. Another, a red-haired seraph, has replaced her, and she too leaves. Then it is a sort of deity, glistening—to tell the truth—so much so that she seems to have fallen from heaven, headfirst, into a barrel of molasses. . . . As each celestial creature passes, Chanel dreams of giving her some earthly attachment, because I hear that low, obstinate voice: 'Take off these *petits machins*. . . . Don't add anything to the décolleté. . . . I want to see the wrist, the neck. . . . Here, look at what I am doing. . . .'

"A pause brings back my attention. Mlle Chanel rests standing up like a thoroughbred horse, even eats this way, eating a *petit pain* with bites that send crumbs flying up to the ceiling—as our ancestors used to say.

"Finally, two dark fires dart at me from under the thick tuft, making me think of the gay humor of the little black bull in a time of recreation. . . . But no. Not yet. Putting down her bread-flute, Chanel lovingly handles some antelope leather, soft, worked, polished, melting, with a fur lining that is still more suave. 'It's for me, that, it's for me! Finally, a garment for me! Oh, how good it will feel to be so warm! A good fur-lined garment that is good and light, very snug. . . .' She closes her eyes and, with a distinctively feminine gesture, presses it against her cheek, the sheared fur and its wild odor, and I begin to intone about slow walks in the winter air and napping in the automobile, all under an antelope coat. With my eyes closed, I can suddenly see two pupils the color of spangled granite. The color of mountain water in the crevices of a rock bathed in sunlight—but Mlle Chanel flatly rejects my suggestions of fur-muffled idleness: 'That? It's to go boar hunting in.'"

△ Colette, in a photograph by Henri Lartigue. Then fifty-three, the author had just bought La Treille Muscate ("The Muscat Arbor") in Saint-Tropez, where she would spend her summers. She had just won kudos for what proved to be her last appearance on the stage. This was in *The Vagabond*, coproduced by the totally bankrupt Poiret. *La Revue de Paris* compared Colette to "a Renoir with luscious arms." But even Goudeket, at first sight, found her *trop en chair* ("too plump"), which in no way prevented his being immediately captivated. Gabrielle Chanel, who had great admiration for Colette, nevertheless took a severe attitude toward the great writer's stoutness: "She positively swaggers in gluttony. The whole of Saint-Tropez is astonished."

The Chanel/Iribe affair and Colette's opinion of it

"*Mon chéri*, what a beautiful day! How can I characterize such weather. One would have to do it in music. So much freshness, warmth, sweetness—who could describe all that?" Colette at Saint-Tropez during grape harvest; Colette the Taurean, with her terrace and the cicadas in her garden; Colette with something of a witch about her and dreadfully abrupt when faced with people who pleased her little—all this is expressed in a letter that she wrote in July 1933 to Maurice Goudeket, the man she had lived with for eight years and would marry two years later. A happy period for Colette. At age sixty, she had found a companion worthy of her and in him, according to her friend Marguerite Moréno, "the possibility of a lovely adventure and perhaps more than a lovely adventure." The time was also a happy one for Chanel, who evidently believed that finally, in the person of Paul Iribe, she had met the man of her life. But Colette had her doubts about Iribe, sensing something demonic in him. "As I was making a purchase at Vachon's, a pair of hands clapped over my eyes, a nice body pressing against my back. . . . It was Misia, full of kisses and tender regards. 'Imagine finding you here!' 'Of course I'm here,' etc. But she had something more urgent for my ear. 'You know, she's marrying him.' 'Who?' 'Iribe. Oh my dear, what an incredible story: Coco's in love for the first time in her life!' Then followed much commentary, etc., etc. 'Oh! I assure you he knows his business, that one.' I didn't have time to ask what business. 'We've been looking for you, even went to your place. We want to take you to dinner in Saint-Raphaël, in Cannes, in . . .' I decline, kiss, and leave with Moune [the wife of the painter Luc Albert-Moreau]. We then went to pick up Kessel [brother of the writer Joseph Kessel] who was buying something or other. Hardly three steps away a pair of arms is thrown about me. They belonged to Le Gaseau [the wife of playwright Henri Bernstein] and her daughter. More protestations of love, etc. 'We've been looking for you. I want to take you to Robert de Rothschild's, to Valescure . . . ,' etc. She already knew I had been named drama critic for the *Journal*. More effusions and kisses. We start out again, Moune and I, only to be stopped a few paces along by yet another embrace. . . . It was the Vals [Valentine Fauchier-Magnan]! 'I've just come from your place, looking for you so that I can take you to dinner at L'Escale with . . . ,' etc. I decline, I decline—repeatedly. Moune and I set off for yet another three steps before my eyes are covered by a new set of hands, this time very fine, cold ones. It was Coco Chanel.

△ *Vendeuses*, mannequins— the whole Chanel team celebrating the feast of Saint Catherine. Gabrielle and Iribe in the back row on the left.

Effusions—of a more reserved order. 'I'm taking you to dinner at L'Escale,' etc. I decline once more, and a little farther along I catch sight of Iribe, throwing me kisses. Then, before I can complete the rite of exorcism, he embraces me, tenderly squeezing my hand between his cheek and shoulder. 'How naughty you are, treating me like a demon!' 'And even then you don't give up?' I say. But he went on overflowing with joy and affection. Altogether he's seen sixty years and twenty springtimes. He is slender, lined, and white-haired, and laughs through a set of brand-new teeth. He coos like a dove, which makes it all the more interesting, because you will find in old texts that demons assume the voice and form of the bird of Venus." Why did Colette dread Iribe so much that she began making the gestures of exorcism as he approached?

"Ça c'est Paris"

par

Jeanne Ramon Fernandez

Bouquet de camélias roses envoyé par Picasso à Mme Errazuriz alors qu'elle gardait la chambre. "Vous tiendrez ce bouquet à la main, lui écrivait Picasso et il complètera le décor charmant que vous savez toujours créer autour de vous"

Ensemble de crêpe Georgette rouge avec toque assortie en feutre et draperie de velours, porté par la Csse Elie de Gaigneron au Thé Rosy organisé par la Marquise de Ganay. A côté d'elle, Mme Santos-Suarez, en noir, porte une toque charmante, fuyante en plumes collées noires

Reçdu d'un paletot de drap rouge bordé de bleu, ce magnifique manghi fait des visites avec sa maîtresse, Mme Paul Gentien, habillée de satin brun avec écharpe de satin rose retenue par un bijou. Feutre brun assorti

Pour recevoir à déjeuner, Madame J.-M. Sert, dans un costume de Georgette noir, de Chanel, porte sa magnifique chaîne de diamants à triple rangs. Un simple tricot de laine rouge, de Chanel également, accompagne cet ensemble

ELLE est intense, captivante, cette vie de Paris, même aux époques où la vie mondaine est au calme plat. Qui dira cet attrait irrésistible de la ville dans laquelle on respire la joie de vivre, où tout au moins on possède ce sentiment réel, absolu, éprouvé nulle part ailleurs : vivre ! Dès le matin, on escompte les rendez-vous, les projets d'aller ici ou là. On sait que la journée ne sera jamais assez étendue pour accomplir tout ce que notre désir a formé.

Cette semaine, où la plupart des gens s'envolent vers le Midi, ce fut pourtant une suite ininterrompue de réunions, de thés, de buts intéressants quotidiens et tout cela dans cette atmosphère intime, charmante, des rues de Paris, de ses places familières, de ses théâtres où nous nous retrouvons chez nous.

Quelle que soit l'affluence prévue dans une fête annoncée longtemps à l'avance, jamais cette affluence ne sera un obstacle au succès d'une soirée. La foule fut incalculable au Bal des Petits Lits Blancs organisé par M. Bailby et jamais soirée ne fut plus gaie ni plus parfaitement réussie que celle-là : rapidité de spectacle, distribution abondante de cadeaux de tous genres, chaque femme regagnant sa voiture, les bras chargés de présents. Toutes les loges, ornées d'une poupée nègre qu'on emportait, étaient remplies de femmes de la haute Société, du monde parlementaire et du monde des riches industriels ; l'effet de la salle était celui des beaux jours d'avant-guerre aussi, les diamants ajoutant leur éclat à celui des girandoles reliant la salle à la scène, c'était un coup d'œil merveilleux.

Dans les premières loges, la Csse E. de Beaumont, la Dsse de Gramont, la Psse d'Arenberg et d'autres parmi les femmes les plus en vue de Paris. Mme Ph. Berthelot avait trois, ambassadeurs dans sa loge et Mme Ganna Walska dans la sienne était ruisselante de brillants.

Misia alone

She was over fifty and no longer the lush young woman who had turned the heads of Bonnard, Vuillard, and Renoir. She had changed; she had suffered. Now it was Gabrielle Chanel who sustained this friend in a trying time just as she had been supported by Misia at an earlier moment. From 1927 through 1929, while Misia agonized through the collapse of her relationship with José-Maria Sert, Chanel took her away from Paris. The two friends could be seen in England and then in Italy. At home, Misia struggled to accommodate the passion her husband had for the young Georgian Roussy Mdivani. For a while their ménage à trois created almost as much astonishment as the famous Colette-Willy-Polaire triangle. In *Venises*, Morand wrote in 1928 of an encounter at the Villa Malcontenta with "Sert, flopped into a sagging armchair and flanked by his two wives stretched out at his feet." But Misia resisted neither a divorce from Sert nor his remarriage. Unhappy but free, she remained as much the

△ Drawing published in 1927 along with this legend: "When receiving for dinner, Mme J.-M. Sert, in a georgette creation by Chanel, wears her magnificent triple-length chain of diamonds. Also by Chanel, the simple red jersey." Mentioned in the same caption was the red overcoat worn by Madame Gentien's Arabian gazelle-hound, dressed, like its mistress, by Chanel.

queen of the artistic world as ever, still gathering about her the legendary masters whose genius she had inspired. When Reverdy sought exile at Solesmes Abbey, it was Misia who enabled him to succeed. When Marcelle Meyer, who had made the music of Les Six known to the world, found herself passing through a difficult period, Misia revived her in 1933 by renting the great hall at the Hôtel Continental and arranging a two-piano concert. While Poulenc turned the pages, the audience followed a program embellished with a quatrain by Max Jacob, who had entitled the poem: A MITIA AMICITIA.

△ Misia, gowned by Chanel for a fête, the "Balloon Ball" given in Sert's studio. She learned to adapt to the period's style without sacrificing what had characterized her throughout the years: a sumptuous Slavitude.

Chanel in Hollywood

In 1929 an unexpected encounter took place. The setting was Monaco and the intermediary, Dimitri of Russia. This descendant of the tsars arranged an introduction between Chanel and Sam Goldwyn, the tsar of Hollywood. Faced with the unprecedented crisis then gripping the United States, Goldwyn wanted to give women renewed reason to go to the movies. In the course of an interview, he disclosed his plan. Women would attend the cinema: "Primo, for the films and the stars; secondo, to see the latest fashions." Thus, Goldwyn had to have Gabrielle Chanel, and he wanted nothing less than to have her make two trips a year to Hollywood. The contract he drew up was to guarantee her a fabulous sum of money: $1 million. This was because the movie mogul wanted the French couturière not only to costume the queens of Hollywood but also to reform their taste. It was a ukase: the gorgeous creatures had henceforth to be dressed exclusively by Chanel in their private lives as well as on the screen. But could the stars be counted on to submit? After long negotiations, Chanel acceded to Goldwyn's wishes and agreed to go to California. Her first visit occurred in April 1931, with Misia Sert going along for the ride. Together, the two Parisians had a triumphant stay in the citadel of cinema.

△ Wearing the same suit as Chanel, Gloria Swanson in *Tonight or Never*, a movie that premiered in December 1931.

▷ Chanel in 1931. From Garbo to Stroheim, from Dietrich to Cukor, everyone felt honored to be involved with her, a woman the local press described as "the greatest mind that fashion has ever known."

Up against the "star system"

Fourteen million Americans were out of work, but
Hollywood went right on, despite the crisis, making films
in colossal studios with casts of thousands. In 1931, the
year that Chanel journeyed to Hollywood, the international dominance of the American cinema rested entirely
upon the "star system," which meant using every means,
at whatever expense, to immortalize the big box-office
draws.

Millions of signed and dedicated photographs kept the
crowds in high fervor and helped generate a climate of
legend around the new idols. Publicity agents took
charge of their loves, their divorces, their mansions, their

△ A Chanel creation Hollywoodized
by Gloria Swanson.

clothes, the better to make them household concerns for an entire nation. Among the stars, there was one of truly magical power: Gloria Swanson. And it was to her that Sam Goldwyn assigned the big role in *Tonight or Never*, a comedy directed by Mervyn Leroy and the first film on which Chanel worked.

Yet, despite an excellent critical reception, Coco left the movie capital of the world and never returned. She could not endure being subordinated to stars who themselves refused to have a style imposed upon them, even the Chanel style. With this outcome, Sam Goldwyn was left holding the bag, but never asked for his money back.

△ Gloria Swanson, dressed by Chanel for *Tonight or Never*, a film in which she played the role of an opera singer who indulged every caprice.

Diamands like none ever seen before

In November 1932 Paris saw the opening of an exhibition of a sort rarely given to a single talent. It involved Chanel and took place in the couturière's own apartment on the ground floor of the Hôtel Pillet-Will in the Faubourg Saint-Honoré. Jewels, all designed by her, were presented on wax busts appropriated from coiffeurs. Made up to perfection, the busts had close surveillance from guards visibly armed with revolvers. The jewelry thus protected was set with diamonds.

It was unheard-of for a woman without experience in jewelry design to presume to work with real gems, especially a woman who had made herself the champion of costume jewelry. Right away, however, it became evident that the real innovation lay in the forms, in the adaptability of the pieces, which could be divided into two or four.

△ She who had persuaded women to wear fake jewelry now launched into the real thing. The idea, it was said, came from Iribe—also the jewelry. It was at the time of the exhibition that Iribe's liaison with Chanel took an official turn. He moved in with her on the Faubourg Saint-Honoré.

Copyright CHANEL 1932.

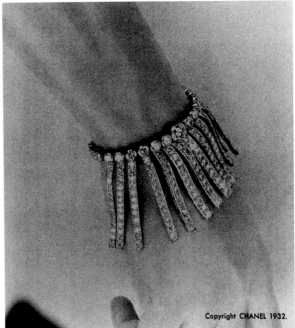

Copyright CHANEL 1932.

△ ◁ A rather baroque piece, a sort of headband forming bangs fit for a Pharaoh's wife.

△ The centerpiece of the exhibition was one of two bracelets that, with the addition of a clip, could be made into a necklace.

◁ Instead of a necklace, Chanel proposed a comet of diamonds. The beautiful photographs in the exhibition catalogue had been made by Robert Bresson.

How to make use of *le beau monde*

A certain notion of luxury

In 1928 Chanel traveled to the heights of Roquebrune and made herself a present of an olive grove and a view of extraordinary beauty overlooking the Mediterranean. A royal acquisition, it consisted of a summer house—her first vacation home. Chanel was then forty-five years old.

Here Chanel sought the natural above all else, thereby affirming her aversion to fussy and facile effects. It was a house in which to live the life of the times. On the inside, it displayed whitewashed walls and few objects. In the garden, under the century-old olive trees, reigned a single color—lavender blue. While her friends sensed a bit of the convent, Chanel declared that she had advised her architect to visit a monastery where, as a child, "she has spent marvelous vacations." In truth, she had sent him to Aubazine, to that orphanage whose severe beauty continued, secretly, to haunt her.

◁ Finished in less than a year, the house—architecture and decoration alike—reflected its creator's habitual rigor. The style of La Pausa would virtually found a school.

△ In the foreground, Duke Fulco di Verdura, Marchese della Cerda was a Sicilian, of very old family, who created remarkable jewelry for Chanel. Behind him: Don Guido Sommi Picenardi, the Marchese di Calvetone, Baron Fabvier, and Count Étienne de Beaumont.

Surrounded by the *crème de la crème*

△ Gabrielle Chanel at La Pausa.

Quotes from Chanel reported by Morand: "I have used society not to flatter my vanity or to humiliate them (I had other means of revenge, just admitting that I sought them out), but, as I said, because they were useful to me and because they circulated about Paris on my behalf. As for myself, I went to bed early. Thanks to them, I kept up with everything, the way Proust, from the depths of his bed, knew what had been said at all the dinners given the night before." Also: "Inasmuch as I seldom went out, it was essential that I be informed of everything that went on in the houses where my clothes were worn. I developed the habit, then unprecedented, of surrounding myself with people of quality so as to establish a link between myself and society. The

287

Russian, Italian, and French aristocracy, English society women—all came and did service in the Rue Cambon." Then Chanel added: "I have never paid idlers." Thus, it is clear that what might appear, at first glance, to be an assembly of parasites was in fact a group of well-known persons chosen and paid by a woman who, born of the people, was completely aware of the lacunae in her social history. The daughter of a Cévenole small-wares peddler counted on the sons of the nobility to initiate her into a style of life that was their birthright but, of course, not hers.

Chanel invents unisex

Putting women into slacks, made possible by the age's liberalization of morals and by the new opportunity in sports available to women of means, constituted the most sensational of the innovations brought about by Chanel. It was she who gave this emulation of masculine attire its

△ Chanel wearing a sailor shirt and wide pajamas made of jersey.

▷ Gabrielle Chanel and her friend from younger days, the opera singer Marthe Davelli.

look of class, and it was she who adapted the style to every occasion, who subjected it to the demands of fashion and varied its interpretations, some sportive and casual, others elegant and refined. Wearing slacks in 1929 was, obviously, a freedom that only rich women could afford. Still, the taboo had been broken, and once the era of leisure and standardized clothing arrived, the Chanel mode had only to go down into the street for pants to become the preference of thousands upon thousands of women. The photographs reproduced here, even though a half-century old, make one feel that the time of the all-purpose jeans is near and that of the androgynous style too. Chanel anticipated those who today consider themselves innovative in their taste for work clothes, such as sailors' pullovers, dockworkers' T-shirts, and the white jackets traditional for plasterers. Before anyone else, she derived fashion from the netherworld of common humanity.

△ Chanel, jacketed and trousered in white duck, with the designer Lucien Lelong in Venice in 1931.

▷ Chanel, Christian Bérard, and Boris Kochno at Monte Carlo in 1932.

△ In 1929 Chanel added to her
haute couture collection a line of
accessories made in wool jersey.
Her matching caps and scarves were
adopted by men (even though not
made for them) just as quickly as
they were by women, and put to use
in a way never actually envisioned
by Chanel—for winter sports.

◁ This photo shows Gabrielle Chanel
in Saint-Moritz in the company of her
friend and collaborator, Étienne de
Beaumont. They are wearing the first
ski togs: shoes that let in water and
pants that twisted uncontrollably.

Chanel leaves her stamp on Saint-Moritz

The first PLM poster designed to promote winter sports appeared in 1900, the period when Switzerland and France were importing the first skis. The poster showed the lady skier dressed in an ankle-length skirt and low-heeled shoes. One year before the outbreak of World War I, Henri Lartigue noted: "Winter sports are not very popular in France." But in the postwar era all this changed quite rapidly. More than any other sport, skiing was a luxury, and the resort that would offer the greatest luxury and at the earliest date was Saint-Moritz. It attracted the wealthy in great numbers from all nations.

△ A toboggan party with the recognizable images of Maria Ruspoli, Duchesse de Gramont, Gabrielle Chanel, Comtesse E. Moretti, and Comtesse de Beaumont.

1929: the "black lady" of the Roaring Twenties sets off her last fireworks

1929: Taste was undergoing some kind of change. Not a decisive shift but a gradual one. At first hardly discernible, it became more pronounced during the social upheavals of 1936 and then continued at full thrust until 1939. Yes, an age had passed. Gone since 1929 was the giddy insolence of the first postwar years, also the craze for black that had characterized both fashion and decoration. The decennials of taste have a way of fixing their own dates in the calendar. The Belle Époque did not open with the century, but in 1899, with the pardon granted to Captain Dreyfus, and ended not in 1910 but in 1914, with the guns of August. Correspondingly, the "Roaring Twenties" did not fall neatly into the 1920–30 decade usually assigned to them. Armand Lanoux assures us: "The twenties. They are the ten years from the demobilization of 1919 to the 'crash' of 1929." Another bizarre thing is that while the new era would have a darker mood, fashion tended toward white.

◁ The whole style of the mad twenties—*les années folles*—had been decreed by Chanel: severe with a preference for black. But a change began to appear in 1926. No more tubular dresses. Slowly, between 1926 and 1929, clothes developed longer lines and greater flair. Here is Chanel's new black dress, as seen by *Vogue*.

△ Drawing in *Vogue*, February 1930: an evening gown by Chanel.

In 1929, while the United States lived through October's "Black Friday," with its stock-market crash and bank closures, Paris, where the economy suffered less and the franc remained stable, entered a decade that for *le beau monde* would prove to be incredibly luxurious, a time of glittering parties attended by women dressed in lustrous white satin. In her preface to the album that Horst entitled *Salute to the Thirties*, Janet Flanner called it "the unexpected apogee of France's rather dowdy Third Republic."

The "white lady" of the thirties

Among the reminiscences of Chanel, as Paul Morand reported them under the title *L'Allure de Chanel*, can be found these highly revealing lines concerning the origin of the vogue for white that suddenly seized the fashionable world in 1929: "I was the first to have rugs dyed

beige. It reminded me of beaten earth. Right away, furnishings all turned beige, until finally the decorators cried for mercy. 'Try white satin,' I said. Whereupon white swamped their ensembles. . . ." Chanel also noted that along with this search for "candid innocence and white satin" came a return to favor of Far Eastern brilliance, bringing white lacquer to walls, Chinese white to vitrines, and white flowers to vases.

A veritable craze for satin

Everywhere satin. Simple or perverse, satin reigned at every level of society as the festive fabric of the thirties. It was in a Mandarin costume made of white satin that the beautiful and formidable Mrs. Reginald Fellowes, one of

△▷ Studies by Drian showing two views of a 1931 dress by Chanel that was most unusual for her. Although the wedding gown normally appeared as the ultimate "bouquet" or the finale of a Paris collection, Chanel had always scorned the rite, declaring she wanted "no circus." Along with Eric, Benito, and Bouché, all of them foreigners, Drian, a lone Frenchman, was counted among the most gifted of the artists who drew dress models in the thirties.

the era's most celebrated hostesses, received her guests at her *hôtel particulier* in Neuilly the evening of a lavish party known as the "Oriental Ball." The daughter of a Franco-Danish Duke and an American mother, "Daisy" Fellowes was as much feared for her sharp wit as she was admired for her stylishness and hospitality. And white satin was again the material when Madame Martinez de Hoz, a South American beauty, appeared as Watteau's Gilles at the "Masterpiece Ball" given by Étienne de Beaumont. Finally, dressed, gloved, and hatted in white satin, the indestructible Mistinguett, then well past sixty, had another triumph on the stage of the Folies-Bergère.

△ The "Queen of the Music Hall," Mistinguett, in *Folies en folies*. Photograph by Horst.

◁ The Honourable Mrs. Reginald Fellowes ("Daisy" to her friends) dressed for her own "Oriental Ball" in a white-satin "Mandarin" costume designed, like the elaborate coiffure, by Coco Chanel. Photograph by Horst.

America and England assign their greatest photographers

Condé Nast, the owner of *Vogue* and *Vanity Fair*, begged Edward Steichen to replace Baron de Meyer, who had departed for the Hollywood studios. Steichen as much as Meyer, and probably in a more decisive way, had been the first to have a real effect on fashion photography, for he was the first to adapt its style to that of avant-garde painting. Indeed, his influence went all the way back to 1900. The enormous salary offered to assure the services of Steichen had no precedent. But this master was quite simply the inventor of fashion photography as a profession and the first photographer to use professional models, such as Marion Morehouse. Signed in 1923, Steichen's contract lasted until 1938, the year in which he abruptly gave up working in fashion. In 1947 Steichen became curator of the Photography Department at New York's Museum of Modern Art.

△ For the dress seen above, Chanel used white organdy. Photograph by Steichen for *Vogue*, 1930.

△ Here, in a 1935 design, Chanel used sequins and tulle. Photograph by Cecil Beaton for *Vogue*.

Cecil Beaton—writer and draftsman of great flair, the-atre designer, ideal companion, adventurous traveler, witty conversationalist, a great and generous spirit—was a protean genius and, until his death, the last in a lost tra-dition, that of the great lords of fashion photography. This distinctively British man was also the quintessential cos-mopolite. He belonged to Paris as much as to New York or even London, and was equally at home in his studio, where a tiny staff adored him, and at the English court, which he served as official portraitist. One of the master's most brilliant successes was the creation of the sets, cos-tumes, and, especially, the hats for the Broadway produc-tion of *My Fair Lady*. In 1925 Beaton perfected the studio technique of posing models against somewhat unreal or poetic environments, doing so with unique elegance.

Chanel poses for Iribe

1933: After twenty-three years of silence, an almost forgotten title, *Le Témoin*, reappeared on the kiosks of France. One might remember, however, that in its first incarnation of 1910 the journal had published an extraordinary caricature of Sarah Bernhardt, which served to introduce a new artist, Jean Cocteau, who signed his work "Jim." Now Iribe was again the director, editorial writer, and principal illustrator of the review, but this time with a publisher in the person of Chanel, who thereby exposed her affair with Iribe to a blaze of publicity. All Paris was talking about it.

Iribe's drawing had lost nothing of its power, fueled by the same corrosive spirit and now, suddenly, exploited on behalf of the most blatant chauvinism. On every page, the sight of France and its grandeur maligned by the world—a Phrygian-capped personification placed in the dock before a sneering tribunal—was enough to rend the soul. But who were the judges? Chamberlain, Hitler, Mussolini, and

△ Portrait of Gabrielle Chanel by Lipnitzki, October 1936.

▷ Drawing by Paul Iribe for *Le Témoin*, 1933.

L'ACCUSÉE

Roosevelt! Throughout the years leading up to World War II Europe's statesmen were constantly on the move, reshuffling alliances and appeasing the arch-villain Hitler. Meanwhile, France stiffened her back and strengthened her military in preparation for the coming onslaught. Hopes rose and fell, but nothing could dim the brilliant social life of Paris. As for Iribe's poor threatened France in the guise of Marianne—this bare-breasted victim half-buried under sod shoveled by a gravedigger named Daladier—she bore an unmistakable resemblance to none other than Chanel.

La France? She is Chanel

And so while France's governments were falling apart with depressing regularity, and rightists were demonstrating daily in the streets, there appeared on the

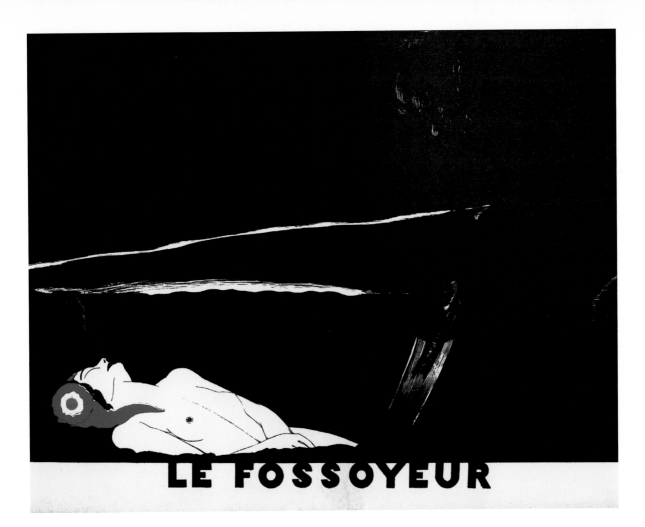

LE FOSSOYEUR

kiosks, displayed among the newspapers, the image of Gabrielle Chanel personifying a crucified France. The vehicle for this performance was, of course, *Le Témoin*, the reactionary review published by Paul Iribe, who made Chanel an instrument through which to exalt values believed to be threatened. For Iribe, Coco became an inexhaustible source of inspiration. Was she proud of being thus chosen? No man before Iribe had so ostentatiously displayed and promoted her.

The rumors concerning Chanel and Iribe proved to be true, which Colette noted in 1933 while writing to Marguerite Moréno: "I have just heard that Iribe is marrying Chanel. Aren't you appalled for Chanel?" Then Colette added: "That man is a most interesting demon."

That Gabrielle Chanel and Paul Iribe would in fact marry was no longer doubted. The beautiful Coco would at last submit to a man.

△ Paul Iribe in 1933.

Coco's revenge

A frenzy of fêtes, marked by a lavishness never seen before, seized high society during the 1930s. The legendary Janet Flanner, Paris correspondent for *The New Yorker*, expressed amazement over these manifestations of dazzling frivolity: "It was then that in Paris a decade of private fêtes and splendid entertainments began in *le beau monde*. . . . In their magnificently furnished Paris mansions *le beau monde* had come into a state of revival brought on by the national prosperity, all the more welcome to them because of its contrast to their previous state of ennui, the social dullness of the pinched postwar years just passed." The "Oriental Ball," the "Circus Ball," the "Forest Ball," the "Masterpiece

◁ Sometimes, and no doubt without realizing it, Chanel revived the attitudes, graces, and coquetries of the café-concert divette. And seeing her in the costume that she made for Valentine Hugo on the occasion of the "Waltz Ball," one cannot help thinking of the young woman on the cover of the song that Chanel made her own during the period when she lit up as a *beuglant* catering to the Moulins garrison.

△ Cover of "Qui qu'a vu Coco?"

Ball," the "Olympia Ball," etc. From May through July, lasting from 1935 until the very height of the summer in 1939, Paris saw an endless stream of masked balls. With Coco Chanel a sought-after guest at every one of them.

At last recognized and invited everywhere, loved, and, according to public rumor, on the verge of marrying Iribe, was Chanel having her revenge and savoring it?

△ Summer 1934. Chanel with Fulco di Verdura at the ball given by Prince Jean-Louis de Faucigny-Lucinge and Baron Nicolas de Gunzburg.

As the war clouds gathered

On January 4, 1935, Pierre Laval went to Rome to sign the Franco-Italian accords, while the French press hailed Mussolini and "his handsome peasant emperor's head." But a few voices of a less lyrical sound could be heard, such as that of the Pope, who said to Ambassador Charles-Roux: "Mussolini tells us he is convinced that war will break out between the English and the Italians and then spread rapidly throughout Europe. He spoke of it all as if he were taking a cup of morning tea." Then there was Léon Blum in *Le Populaire*: "For the first time a French minister is a guest of the murderer of Matteoli. . . ." In fact, the agreement was signed only at the price of a debasement. What price? A free hand for "Il Duce" in Ethiopia. Rome rejoiced, for Fascist Italy could now pursue its war with no further delay. Less than a month later, a contingent of the Italian army set off for Ethiopia. When Haile Selassie, Menelik's grandson who had become Negus and then Emperor in 1930, saw his country so threatened, he

△ As in every spring, 1935 saw the ball given by Count Étienne de Beaumont, who was by far the liveliest and most elegant person there. His theme this year? France's *Grand Siècle*—the Age of Louis XIV. Serge Lifar attended as the dancer Vestris, wearing a costume made by Chanel.

△ At Étienne de Beaumont's masked ball, Chanel impersonating Watteau's *Indifférent*.

appealed for help to the League of Nations, a body the Ethiopian war would destroy. On October 3, 1935, Italy invaded Ethiopia, bringing Haile Selassie's denunciation of the bombings and the massacres of women and children. By May 3, 1936, the Italians had entered Addis Ababa. Soon, the war would take other turns and spread like wildfire to the rest of the world.

. . . Paris rushed from party to party

In Paris the summer of 1935 was a time when Gabrielle Chanel, the gifted costume designer, and the stage designer Christian Bérard, whom fashionable women fought over for advice, were both dream merchants to a senseless society. They were the craftsmen of countless metamorphoses, the magicians of a shadowy theatre whose denizens spent the night until dawn pretending to be someone else. For Chanel, however, 1935 also brought the summer when, one August day at La Pausa, Paul Iribe fell dead on the tennis court before her very eyes. With this she entered a long and cruel solitude.

The Popular Front

Spring 1936: In a country fraught with crisis, where severe poverty gripped the working class, where the price of grain fell to half that of 1929, where bankruptcies doubled, where unemployment continued to increase, a bitter election campaign got underway. But on April 26, 1936, it rained all over France. It rained hard, and as the water poured down, it seemed to bring hope to certain people. Nothing would change, for who had the courage to go out and vote in such weather? As it turned out, however, 85 percent of the electorate went to the polls, bringing a victory for the Popular Front. The immense and resounding defeat of the right momentarily drowned out the noise over the German victory in the Saar plebiscite. Seized by fear, the wealthy classes locked their doors and bought gold. France, for the first time in its history, had at the head of its government a socialist and a Jew to boot. This was Léon Blum, the nation's most maligned man. "He should be shot," said the writer Maurras, "but in the back."

△ While unprecedented negotiations were underway between employers as a group and salaried workers, Léon Blum the socialist and Maurice Thorez the communist met and shook hands, to the sound of an extended acclamation.

June 1936: women too . . .

"Inconceivable, unimaginable, inadmissable." Such were the terms with which *les patrons* ("bosses") reacted to the wave of strikes that rolled across France in May. Soon, fear would be succeeded by—and the word is not too strong—terror. The explosion, which gathered force as it swelled, took on an unpredictable and thus doubly rebellious character. First of all, there was the general atmosphere: "The good humor of the strikers is the most sinister of all the omens," reported *L'Écho de Paris*. That relaxed, happy, and determined mood had the effect of a body blow. The second surprise came when the women joined the movement en masse, which left all observers in a state of indescribable stupefaction. With their *demoiselles* occupying the premises day and night, shops and department stores fell into utter disarray. That salesgirls should dance to the accordion and applaud the secretary general of the CGT (France's biggest labor union federation) just as much as Mistinguett, who appeared to sere-

△ May 1936: The Popular Front organized a demonstration in homage to those who had died for the 1871 Commune. Sculptors and writers, painters and composers mobilized en masse and joined in a march. La Maison de la Culture de Paris, founded in 1935, created the first posters, saluting Daumier, Molière, Zola, etc. The year 1936, therefore, marked an important breakthrough, in which aristocratic culture ceded some ground to the rise of popular creativity.

nade them at dawn, all taking place behind the locked doors and under the glass domes of those temples of commerce, Printemps and the Galeries Lafayette—here then, truly, was revolution.

△ Refreshments served under the lowered iron curtain of a couture atelier.

◁ At the Galeries Lafayette, the striking employees were visited by Léon Jounaux, secretary general of the CGT.

At the House of Chanel: timidly lifted fists

An unspeakable gesture—the staff at Chanel's went on strike! One June morning at opening time a smocked apprentice pasted a placard on the entrance announcing that the premises had been "occupied." Along with this was attached a standard cardboard box, decoratively tied with ribbons but slit like a ballot box to permit the passing public to support the cause with contributions. Next, a group of delegates appeared at the Ritz, where Chanel lived, and requested an audience with *la patronne*. Such a thing would have been unthinkable a fortnight before. Now, submission and constraint had come to a sudden end.

Mademoiselle let it be known that, not knowing what a "delegate" was, she could not receive one, but that she

would see her workers in her own time at the Chanel salon. She dressed with care, putting on her triple-length rope of pearls, and presented herself at the portal of her *maison de couture*, where the delegates blocked all access. Chanel was on the steps of her own house, and her employees refused to obey her! It was an affront that she would long remember and resent.

That women, by means of a strike, should seek to assert themselves, in a country where salaries were outrageously low and job insecurity was total, simply outraged Chanel, who would not tolerate such behavior. Thus, negotiations between Gabrielle and her staff began in a climate of high tension. She turned a deaf ear even to the most legitimate demands: employment contracts, weekly salaries, limited working hours, paid vacations. To that Chanel responded with the mass firing of three hundred employees—who refused to budge. Things dragged on until her advisors indicated that if an

agreement were not reached soon, there would be no hope of presenting an autumn collection. Finally, Mademoiselle gave in. This was undoubtedly one of the rare occasions in her long career when Gabrielle Chanel failed to conceal her deep consternation. Iribe was dead. Her business was all she had. She was alone in the world, alone in the face of rebellion.

△ A picket line at the entrance to the Chanel workrooms. Apprentice dressmakers and saleswomen block the entrance, to which they have hung a shoebox slit open for contributions and a placard announcing their occupation of the premises.

1936: to the seashore

France was the last country in Europe to recognize the right of salaried employees to rest. Suddenly, panic struck the boardwalks of Deauville. Paid vacations had the effect of forcing the privileged classes to suffer the sight and sound of an unheard-of race—workers—who, with entire families, happily invaded the Normandy coast.

During this period of revolt and near revolution, Gabrielle Chanel went to dinner at the house of friends on the Avenue Foch. Her chauffeur took her there in her Rolls Royce, which had particularly elegant suede upholstery. The chauffeur went off to have a glass of wine and a light supper, leaving the car parked on the elegant avenue. He had, unfortunately, forgotten to lock the door, and a rebellious passerby put a dog turd on the back seat. When Chanel discovered it, she was briefly outraged, but immediately started thinking how to adapt fashion to these new times.

△ On the boardwalk in 1936: workers arriving on their first "paid vacations."

▷ On the boardwalk in 1930: Kees van Dongen, called "Kiki," the painter upon whom society women doted.

Chanel/Visconti

A beautiful name, a splendid fortune, and a handsome physique. These were, when he met Chanel, the only assets of Luchino Visconti. In the circles where he moved, his passion for literature appeared most unusual. Moreover, he had a predilection for authors never heard of in his world. Scion of one of Italy's noblest families, the Visconti di Modrone, he seemed to embody a rather cruel contradiction. If aristocratic traditions, luxury, sumptuousness, and certain privileges remained incomparably fascinating for him, he was no less sensitive to the causes of their inevitable disappearance. Even though Visconti felt no sense of caste, the certainty of his class's decline obsessed him. And all the nobility to which Visconti had been born made him perceive this heritage as a "paradise lost," a feeling that was continually at odds with its possessor's desire for social justice.

△ Luchino Visconti in 1936.

▷ Jean Renoir, the actor, with Nora Grégor in *La Règle du jeu (The Rules of the Game)*, 1939, directed by Jean Renoir and costumed by Chanel.

Chanel/Renoir

Chanel conquered Visconti. He invited her to Italy and there presented her to his father, who also fell under the Frenchwoman's charm. And it was at the height of the Popular Front that Gabrielle succeeded in persuading Jean Renoir to allow Luchino Visconti to watch him make a film. Renoir had finished *La Vie est à nous*, a propaganda film commissioned by the Communist Party, and was then working on *Les Bas-Fonds* (*The Lower Depths*), based upon the play by Maxim Gorky and starring Jean Gabin and Louis Jouvet. Renoir not only accepted into the studio the presence of an Italian aristocrat with the bearing of a *condottiere*, but, shortly thereafter, even took him on as an assistant. And it was with him that Renoir made *Une Partie de campagne*, thereby opening the doors of a future for Visconti.

◁ It was the day after Munich that Renoir, still glowing from the success of *La Grande Illusion*, approached Chanel and asked her to do the costumes for his next film. "We are going to try to make a happy picture. This has been a life-long ambition of mine," declared Renoir. What emerged was *La Règle du jeu* (*The Rules of the Game*). The subject? An upperclass woman deceived by her husband. Would she in turn be unfaithful to him and with whom? The drama develops when the heroine is courted by a famous aviator of modest means, for the rule of this shadowy game is that members of the aristocracy may not ally themselves with anyone from without. But the rule must be applied suavely; thus, the intruder will be shot like a rabbit by a jealous gamekeeper. A fortuitous accident allowing the murder to be judged inadvertent and the whole affair smoothed over. Chanel's costumes expressed to perfection what was a cruel paraphrase of *Les Caprices de Marianne*, a scathing image of château life in the 1930s. Now Chanel found herself linked to the fate of Renoir's most ambitious and pessimistic film. Not only was the picture booed, it was even banned. In 1939, the year the film appeared, the military censors deemed it "demoralizing." Disgusted, Renoir left France forever and took up residence in the United States.

For *Oedipus Rex*
costumes that created a scandal

In 1937, designing for the theatre continued to occupy Chanel, as it did without interruption until the declaration of war, undoubtedly because, of all her tasks, this one proved most effective in dispelling her loneliness and depression. Jean Cocteau dominated the theatre, fashion, and taste of Paris in these years. And since it was from Cocteau that a group of young, unknown actors wanted an adaptation of *Oedipus Rex*, an ancient drama never before given in modern times, Chanel received the commission for costumes. She was very popular with the actors and designed a strange interlacement of mummylike wrappings, which the critics found to be of a rare indecency.

△ Iya Abdy, a Russian of great beauty, was a member of the *Oedipus Rex* company. For a necklace, she wore spools of thread all strung together in a double row, thus completing the superb costume designed by Chanel. With this production began a loyal and enduring friendship between Chanel and Abdy.

△ The debut of an unknown:
the actor Jean Marais.

III. Mademoiselle Chanel

"I don't like people talking about the Chanel fashion,
Chanel—above all else, is a style.
Fashion, you see, goes out of fashion. Style never."

Coco Chanel

Chanel's finest years

The two rivals

The thirties saw the rise of a new prima donna of haute couture. This was Elsa Schiaparelli, a Roman lady of a well-to-do family that had produced such illustrious men of learning as a great astronomer, for whom a street in Rome was named, and an archaeologist who had located the site of the first tomb in Egypt's Valley of the Kings. But not only was Elsa a person of solid background; she also had a lively intelligence and native originality, all of which endowed her work with a quality as mad as it was provocative. By bringing a new tone to elegance, she threatened the primacy of Chanel. Soon the competition between the two women would become an unremitting vendetta. Schiaparelli began with only a small group of women as her clients, women who, far from wishing to promote her talent, preferred to remain the only ones aware of it—the only ones who knew where to obtain the most amusing little sweaters in Paris.

In 1927, however, Schiaparelli emerged from anonymity after *Vogue* declared one of her creations "the sweater

◁ Portrait of Elsa Schiaparelli, Chanel's great rival in the 1930s. Photograph by Horst, 1936.

△ A Schiaparelli dress sketched by Christian Bérard for *Vogue*, 1936.

of the year," thereby launching what would become a great career. Nevertheless, until 1933 Chanel remained largely unrivaled. Parisian haute couture, like high fashion, constituted an empire in which the power was held by women of great renown, such as Vionnet, Lanvin, Alix, the Callot sisters, and Louise Boulanger, each of whom had her following. Suddenly this peaceable kingdom found itself troubled once "Schiap," as she was called, truly arrived, upsetting the balance of power.

△ Portrait of Chanel made by Horst in 1936, at the height of the Chanel/Schiaparelli rivalry. Chanel, still smarting from Madeleine Vionnet's habit of calling her "that milliner," would always refer to Schiaparelli as "the Italian," and never once pronounced her name.

23 Schiaparelli

1936

21 Chanel
74

A B Vg

Chanel
Taffetas noir

Schiaparelli
Tweed bleu-marine

Bérard

Schiaparelli and Chanel, although totally different in their tastes, were the same kind of woman. Schiaparelli as well enjoyed glamorous friendships. Indeed, her embroideries were conceived by Salvador Dalí. And she reinforced her cause from surprising quarters. Thus, her necklaces were the work not of some Grand Duchess (which by then would hardly have been original) but by a young Russian much admired by *le Tout-Montparnasse*. She too was called Elsa, and her lover, a certain Louis Aragon, the poet, took charge of Schiaparelli's deliveries. He could be found running up and down the stairs *chez* "Schiap," his arms loaded with female finery. In sum, the friend of the Surrealists was now taking on the friend of the Cubists. The fashion press, which gleefully reported the beginnings of the sort of confrontation that has always delighted Paris, increasingly compared Schiap's dresses with those of Chanel.

△ Chanel in 1938 with her stable of mannequins, all coiffed in the same manner as *la patronne* and dressed by her in elegant smocks.

◁ Schiaparelli and Chanel dresses drawn by Christian Bérard for *Vogue* in 1936 and 1937. Bérard, fresh from the success of his sets and costumes for *La Machine infernale* (Cocteau's play based upon the Oedipus legend), divided his time as best he could between the rival couturières.

A court of portrait photographers

At age fifty-five, Gabrielle Chanel was in the prime of her beauty. Her features, like her figure, had reached their ultimate refinement. And never had she dressed with more invention or with greater perfection. Never had she been more admired, or more invited. Making an appearance became an obligation, for she had to show herself in order to deal with the competition. Elsa Schiaparelli was hard on her heels. Chanel decided to create and reign over a veritable court of photographers. They proved to be more than interested in her face: they were passionate about it.

△▷ Two portraits of Gabrielle Chanel made by Cecil Beaton in the subject's home around 1935.

◁ Chanel and Christian Bérard were photographed in the Italian Pavilion the day it was inaugurated in 1937 at the Paris Exposition des Arts et Techniques.

◁◁ Gabrielle Chanel photographed in 1935 by George Hoyningen-Huene. This extraordinary portrait stands apart from all other known images of Chanel. Is it because of the contrast between the modernity of the face and the classically Spanish look of the lace ruff? By this time Hoyningen-Huene, a thirty-five-year-old Russian aristocrat, had made a modest start as a designer for a small dressmaking concern owned by his sister and had even attempted to paint in the manner of André Lhote. Then he came to the notice of Edna Woolman Chase, the close collaborator of the all-powerful Condé Nast, the publisher of *Vogue*. Once engaged in 1925 as the permanent Paris representative of American *Vogue*, he soon emerged as one of the principal stars of that publication. Hoyningen-Huene was a curious man, sometimes exploding with imagination, then sometimes sinking into deep melancholy. Born in St. Petersburg to a Baltic baron and an American mother, he was consumed by a veritable passion for France and Paris. But when war broke out, he became convinced that Europe was finished forever. By 1946 this quintessential European had taken up residence in Hollywood, where he spent his time as a color coordinator for George Cukor and other film directors and as a teacher of photography. There he died in 1968.

At the center of the artistic life of her time

△ Les Ballets de Monte-Carlo, supported by American financiers, beneficiary of patronage from the commune of Monte Carlo, and directed by René Blum, was the only dance company that came to the aid of Diaghilev's troupe. By 1932 it could boast the presence of a number of dancers formerly with the Ballets Russes, along with Diaghilev's choreographers and collaborators, among them Alexandra Danilova, Woizikowski, Kochno, Balanchine, and Massine. In 1938 Monte Carlo witnessed the creation of Massine's choreography set to Beethoven's Seventh Symphony, with designs by Christian Bérard, as well as Massine's *La Gaieté parisienne*, danced against sets by Étienne de Beaumont. It was a triumphant season. After the opening, celebrities gathered at a supper given by Prince de Faucigny-Lucinge. Left to right: Alexandra Danilova, who starred in *La Gaieté parisienne*, Salvador Dalí, Gabrielle Chanel, and Georges Auric.

△ After the dress rehearsal of *Le Corsaire*, during a supper given by Misia Sert, Anne Marie-Laure de Noailles, Igor Stravinsky, Vera de Bosset Sudeikin, whom the composer would marry in 1940, and Gabrielle Chanel.

◁ May 1938: In the wings of the Théâtre de l'Athénée, following the dress rehearsal of Marcel Achard's *Le Corsaire*, a play directed by Louis Jouvet and designed by Christian Bérard, Gabrielle Chanel and Serge Lifar congratulate Jouvet. Notable features of Coco's attire are the heavy white crepe of the dress and the mixture of real and fake jewelry.

CHANEL   CHANEL

Such was fashion
during the last summer of dancing

1938: Chanel's prestige had never been higher. The couturière suffered no damage from the competition offered
by Schiaparelli; indeed, she met it point for point. When
her rival launched, to great fanfare, a new color—"shocking pink"—Chanel introduced her irresistibly seductive
gypsy style. It delighted America, along with the best of
French and foreign artists, whose drawings appeared to
great effect in all the magazines.

But however brilliant the evening dresses, they would
have a brief life. Once war had been declared in 1939, all
such frippery disappeared. Meanwhile, the neat and
attractive daytime wear of that year endured, practically
unchanged, throughout the occupation, as if in that triste
period fashion wanted to preserve the happy impression
of Europe's last moment of peace.

△ While Schiaparelli was cutting off
slacks at midcalf, Chanel still objected
to anything that did not fall in a
straight line, like the classic suit for
men. Here a black, belted blouse, with
pants and jacket in printed cotton.
Drawing by Bérard for *Vogue*, 1937.

△◁ A tricolor number, the last
evening dress presented by Gabrielle
Chanel before the declaration of war
and the closing of her house.
Drawing by Eric for *Vogue*, 1939.

◁ Gypsy dresses by Chanel. "In Paris,
le sex-appeal is the principal theme of
all the new collections," wrote the
English edition of *Vogue*, adding that
for daytime the waist was in and well
cinched, whereas for evening
everything was fire and flames, thanks
to the craze for sequins, which
proliferated all over bodices, boleros,
and skirt bottoms. Finally, one read
that the hats were all perfectly
ridiculous, with the exception of those
made of faille ribbons, and these were
the last word in chic. Sketch by
Bouché for *Vogue,* 1938.

The summer of disaster

It all began on May 10. The barometer registered fine weather. Flowers were in full bloom and the trees loaded with blossoms. A spring day like any other.

Everything ended in a railway car at Rethondes on June 21, 1940, the first day of summer, when the armistice was signed following the worst defeat that France had ever suffered.

△ This disarmed Frenchman, with his fixed stare and stricken expression, presented the desperate face of defeat, made worse by the mockery of a passing German.

△ The day the Wehrmacht entered Paris. June 14, 1940.

Meanwhile, the Low Countries had been invaded and by May 15 the Dutch army knocked out. Before capitulation, Weygand had replaced the easygoing Gamelin in the French high command. Belgium fell on May 28. After their entrapment at Dunkirk, the British finally managed to escape from France. Mussolini entered the war on June 10. At dawn on June 14 a deserted Paris, evacuated by the government and declared an open city, saw the arrival of the first troops of the Wehrmacht.

Before the armistice of June 21 was signed, in the very railway car where Foch had put his signature to the 1918 Armistice, something historic happened. In a solemn message, Churchill had offered the Bordeaux government an almost complete fusion of the French and British nations, a community of forces, interests, and rights. Premier Paul Reynaud, following the advice of his Generals—Pétain and Weygand—rejected the offer.

The lion of Great Britain

On June 17, the morning after the message from Churchill, that man of experience, Léon Blum, sat in a modest hotel and tried to convince certain members of the government that the honor of France would rise again if the metropolitan government could be resettled abroad, and if immediately a new commander in chief could be named, a person of whom, Blum said, "one could expect faith and that heroic judgment, as Retz put it, capable of distinguishing the extraordinary from the impossible." At Bordeaux no one had any interest in Blum's ideas. But on June 18 a new appeal, this one signed by Charles de Gaulle, proved that such a man existed. Everything thereafter would depend upon Great Britain. Attacked without respite on land and sea, subjected to furious bombardments and ravaged in all its cities, Britain would not give way. Thus the war, which most Frenchmen (and most Americans as well) considered lost, was in reality only beginning.

△ What did Gabrielle Chanel think of the role played by Winston Churchill in the European tragedy? She had known the great man since 1924. A friend from her golden years, always an admirer, and closely associated with Bend'or, Duke of Westminster, Churchill had now become the savior of Great Britain. Here he is in 1928, hunting near Dieppe with Chanel and his son Randolf.

The German tactic consisted of redoubling the nightly raids on London and the threats by radio. The Reich predicted the end of England by October 1940. The gamble did not pay off. Churchill, who was far from having control of the air, announced that the day would come when the reprisals of the RAF would be even more terrible. This indeed came to pass. And until the end of the war it was Churchill who carried the hopes of the free world. In 1954, on his eightieth birthday, Churchill assured the British people that he had done nothing but express their own will. "You were the real lions," he said, "I simply roared."

△ Winston Churchill, during a visit to a bombed-out section of London, is cheered by the working population.

1940: France with its arms raised

On July 10, in the frivolous setting of the Grand Casino at Vichy, which had been hastily transformed into a suitable legislative palace, the parliamentary democracy signed its own death warrant. "It should dissolve in order to make way for an authoritarian regime," Pierre Laval declared. A purely formal body, the assembly acquiesced.

La Claque lavalienne—as Blum called it—took care to muffle the voices of those deputies who kept alive some semblance of opposition: "The public boxes and galleries had been packed by Doriot. . . . Because he occupied the city with the same authority as the militia. On leaving the casino one found oneself passing by howling mobs who launched their furious outrage or fierce acclamation at anyone they recognized."

At the end of the session, France had a new regime, resulting not from a vote but imposed by the will of the occupier and those in league with him. At its head stood an old man who arrogated all power to himself: Marshal

△ Marshal Pétain in Lyon. The tour he made in the autumn of 1940, which included almost every large city in the free zone, was a series of triumphs. In Lyon, on November 18, the members of the legion took the oath en masse.

Pétain. His first constitutional act was to designate an heir presumptive: Laval. Pétain found his warmest adherents among the veterans of 1914–18. And from this sector came the legion that swore their loyalty out loud wherever the Marshal went. Right away the haute bourgeoisie ranged itself on the side of Vichy. With the exception of a few isolated dissenters, all continually threatened with denunciation and treated as hooligans and traitors, France in 1940 devoted itself to the cult of Marshal Pétain. Thus, Vichy—during and after World War II—became synonymous with defeat and collaboration with the occupying Nazis, still a subject of discussion, disagreement, and bitterness.

△ The return of *l'Aiglon*. On December 11, Laval conveyed to Pétain an invitation from Hitler to attend the ceremony marking the return to Paris of the ashes of the "Eaglet," the son of Napoleon I and Marie-Louise of Austria. Only De Brinon, delegate of the French government in the Occupied Zone—a grotesque figure clutching his violets—would be at the Invalides to receive the remains with a Nazi salute. The next morning, Paris made an ironic suggestion: "Less ashes, and more coal," which infuriated Otto Abetz, Ambassador from the Reich.

Elegance for what?
Haute couture for whom?

From 1940 to 1941, a time when everyone thought Hitler would win the war, a certain contingent of *le Tout-Paris* joined the collaboration as if it were the natural thing to do. At the start of the occupation, the German soldiers were instructed to be on their best behavior, and the High Command set themselves up in the lap of luxury at the Ritz, paying their bills in scrap money. The Lutetia was the headquarters of the Gestapo, and at the elegant Bristol on the Faubourg St. Honoré, the American expatriate Florence Gould continued her literary lunches, now with the addition of a few German officers. In Fabre-Luce's *Journal de la France* one could read: "The green uniform is, after all, the latest novelty that Paris, in its natural curiosity and frivolity, is trying to tame."

With the exception of Chanel, who closed her salon immediately after war was declared, the couturiers of Paris went right on presenting two collections a year. Wool and silk had disappeared, but even with ersatz materials, haute couture worked wonders.

◁ Elegance ca. 1941. A full-skirted coat permitted the wearer to travel by bicycle. Completing the ensemble were a shoulder-strap bag, a shopping basket on the handlebars, low boots with imitation felt and cork soles, and a hat enveloped in a cloud of veiling.

△ In 1942 the haute couture trade association decided to take the spring collections to the Free Zone for presentation not only to German and Italian buyers but also to Swiss and Spanish ones. Shown here is the arrival of the star designers: Jeanne Lanvin, Marcel Rochas, and Jacques Fath.

◁△ No restrictions for the milliners, who were exempted from textile rationing. Illustrated is a wartime creation by Jeannette Colombier.

△ Chanel at the opening of an exhibition of paintings by Cassandre. With her is Serge Lifar, who, from his post at the Opéra, dominated the world of dance. Anticipating a German victory, Göring proposed Lifar as director of the future European Ballet. Even Hitler saw fit to receive the great dancer.

◁ A fashion show at the Théâtre des Célestins.

The humiliation

On August 25, 1944, the surrender of General von Choltitz confirmed General Leclerc's victory. It meant the end of street fighting and the beginning of great fear among the guilty—of revenge, of the settling of accounts, and of summary executions. Liberation left France divided, between the excommunicators and the excommunicated, or those vulnerable to being so. And for several months, during which the Resistance and the new authority struggled to halt excesses and violence, the nation teetered on the brink of civil war.

For some two weeks after that morning on August 26, 1944, when General de Gaulle and leaders of the Resistance marched under a brilliant sun from the Arc de Triomphe to Notre-Dame, sometimes to the roar of applause, sometimes to the crack of gunfire—order remained an agonizing problem and the danger of insurrection very great. How could it have been otherwise in a city left to itself, where the police now found themselves

△ A German fallen into the hands of the very enemies he most feared: the FFI.

346

△ All across France the same scene repeated itself: a witch-hunt for collaborators and women who had submitted to the occupiers. Here a woman is led nude through the streets of Paris by a throng of jeering men.

identified with the dispossessed, where those formerly in authority were now destitute and often under arrest, where the new authority had not yet gained credibility, where—worst of all—undesirable elements had introduced themselves into the ranks of the insurgents and, under the guise of resistance, were in the process of settling old scores.

It was in this dark atmosphere that Chanel was apprehended in September of 1944. Many years later she would still all but choke with fury when recalling the day two men arrived at the Ritz and unceremoniously demanded that she follow them forthwith. The order for her arrest came from the Committee of Public Morals. One can imagine the alarm that ran through her entourage. A few hours later, however, Chanel was released and allowed to return to the Ritz. Thus, it must be said that relative to what was inflicted upon those who had embraced a policy of collaboration, or to the popular wrath imposed upon women who had become romantically involved with Germans, Gabrielle experi-

enced a very slight hell. She was not paraded nude through the streets, nor was her head shaved and her brow marked with a swastika.

Shortly thereafter, moreover, Chanel managed to reach Switzerland without difficulty. She would remain there eight years, an exile who returned to France only for brief visits. Then, less than two years later, she was even permitted to go to the United States. This was indeed surprising, because for a very long time, visa requests for America received the most careful scrutiny. Chanel, however, had no more problem making this new trip in 1947 than she had had in going to Switzerland in 1945.

△ Chanel in an eloquent, if damning, portrait made in 1948 by the young American photographer Richard Avedon.

Obviously, protection from the top had assured her a liberty that others, a good deal less culpable than she, did not enjoy.

The day after Liberation, an implacable order from the highest places had, in one stroke, kept Chanel from being purged. To whom did she owe this impunity? It is thought, without absolute certainty, to have been the intervention of the Duke of Westminster with his friend Winston Churchill that made Chanel the beneficiary of a consideration known to no other person in those troubled days.

A trap set by Richard Avedon

In 1948 a young American photographer was beginning to make a reputation for himself. For the second time, his reports on the Paris collections, published in *Harper's Bazaar*, had, quite rightly, been judged both innovative and important. The young man in question attended the fashion shows, still as a statue, at the side of his formidable editor in chief, Carmel Snow. This was Richard Avedon, and he took advantage of his trip to Paris to look up Chanel. The designer was then making a brief stop in the Rue Cambon, a figure tragically on the sidelines of everything. There were many who, mindful of her wartime behavior, refused to speak to the great couturière. Chanel lived as if in quarantine, which made her all the more happy to see the foreign photographer who appeared and asked her to pose for him. Although meeting Avedon for the first time, Chanel knew him well from his published work.

Avedon had found a wall pasted over with two posters that, given the presence of Chanel, constituted one of those telling contrasts for which he already knew the secret. Coco, without suspecting the trap this pitiless young man had set for her, stood before the wall. One poster asked "Why Hitler?"; the other carried the date "1848"—that revolutionary year—and, under the face of the French Republic, which Chanel herself had personified in Iribe's drawings, the words: "Liberty, Equality, Fraternity." Then Avedon, having made his damning portrait, did the elegant thing and refused to publish it during the subject's lifetime.

△ Richard Avedon, born in Manhattan of Russian parents, dreamt of becoming a writer, but, after war broke out, he joined the Marines as a photographer in the identity-card service. Come the peace, he took up fashion photography under the tutelage of Alexei Brodovitch, the most celebrated of all art directors. Hired by *Harper's Bazaar* in 1945, Avedon quickly became the magazine's star photographer. His move to *Vogue* in 1965 hit the fashion community like an earthquake. In the photograph above—made by Henri Cartier-Bresson—Avedon is seen with Carmel Show, editor of *Harper's Bazaar*, and Marie-Louise Bousquet.

△ A German officer shared Chanel's life during and after the Occupation. Here he is before the war, when he called himself an embassy attaché, but in fact was in Paris as the director of propaganda for the Reich. His name: Hans Gunther von Dincklage.

Bérard

Christian Dior
La ligne corolle
Jaquette cintrée en shantung
jupe longue finement plissée.

1947: the Dior bombshell

On February 12, 1947, during a glacial, coal-starved winter, a forty-two-year-old designer (whom only a few knew as the *modéliste* at Lelong from 1942 to 1946)—a rank newcomer named Christian Dior—presented to a wonderstruck audience a series of creations that would revolutionize every principle of modern dress for women. The continuing prewar style—with its skirt length fixed just below the knee, its straight lines accentuating neither the hips nor the bust, its padded shoulders, all dating from 1939 and adapted to conditions imposed by the Occupation—disappeared in one stroke. Skirts dropped twenty centimeters to a level below the calf. Shoulders not only shed their squareness and padding but actually became as soft and delicate as possible. Straight lines were replaced by a wasp waist that set off the bust, which, like the hips, assumed a fullness that skillful stiffening emphasized still further.

From these changes came the silhouette the English-speaking press immediately dubbed the "New Look,"

△ In a gray salon with Proustian decorations, a timid unknown, surrounded by his staff of female directors, prepares his collection: Christian Dior.

◁ The suit that scored a hit, by Dior. Christian Bérard immortalized the creation in this sketch made for *Vogue*, which published the image full page in the June 1947 issue.

signifying the "womanly woman" (*femme-femme*), a look launched by Christian Dior in an atmosphere of excitement and euphoria. This was justified by the professionalism of the work, the perfect cutting and finish of the clothes, the sheer wealth of material (some fifteen meters for a daytime dress, twenty-five for an evening gown), and the rustle of rediscovered petticoats. Also contributing to the enthusiasm was the devastating beauty of the mannequins, who accepted the stupefaction they aroused with aloof, almost absent-minded expressions, sweeping along whole ranks of spectators as if by the very grace of their movements and gestures they could dispel all the gloom of the postwar period, a time of rationed milk, bread, wine, and sugar, of chronic strikes and soaring inflation.

The Paris papers were on strike the day after the birth of the New Look, with the result that the bomb first exploded abroad, where it became front-page news. On a sofa that was to become famous sat the Sacred Monsters of Fashion: Helene Lazareff, director of *Elle*; Madame Castanier from the Officiel de la Couture; and Carmel Snow, who was the legendary director of *Harper's Bazaar*. It was Snow who

△ Christian Dior in 1947. By going against the reasonable, by opting for the contrary of what was expected of a nation ruined by years of foreign occupation, Christian Dior, that cultivated bourgeois, that son of sober Normandy who long hesitated between a career in government and the management of an art gallery, became a couturier and in this capacity returned Paris to its position of leadership in the world of both fashion and textiles. Backing the unknown Dior was Marcel Boussac, the formidably rich and powerful industrialist whose investment in the genius that created the New Look was substantial. Together they would realize a historic success and place the Dior stamp on the entire free world.

wrote that here was a new look, in fact giving a name to this fashion revolution. The Dior collection scored an immediate hit, which brought a veritable tidal wave of buyers and individual clients into the Avenue Montaigne. The success arrived, moreover, despite the reactions of certain American interests eager to save, through hostile articles, inventories worth millions, which the New Look would nonetheless render obsolete. Women's organizations in the United States even called on Dior to cease his "indecencies."

In England Sir Stafford Crips, the Minister of Economic Affairs, expressed indignation and insisted that the country maintain a short-skirt style conforming to common sense and the rigorous restrictions still in effect. But all such efforts proved futile, for when the French ambassador to London held a private showing, the two royal Princesses themselves applauded the works of Christian Dior, almost in unison with France's commerce minister and the man in the street, all of whom rejoiced over the triumph of *le nioulouk*.

△ At Dior's, a stairway packed with journalists. Each collection was an event attracting an enormous crowd. Even the press joined in the chorus of praise and applause. Here, behind a fan, is Emilio Terry, the architect, in a private exchange with Mme de Semont, reporter for *Le Monde*.

Comeback for an old lady

1954: Dior's triumph could only make Chanel seem all the more forgotten. It simply confirmed the fact that a radical change had taken place and that nothing could bridge the gap left by such a long absence. Whereas prewar couture had been entirely dominated by women—Lanvin, Schiaparelli, Vionnet, Alix—it now fell into the hands of men—Balenciaga, Dior, Piguet, and Fath, among others. It was an ineluctable revolution, and Chanel, whose couture house had been closed for fifteen years, felt herself afloat in an endless "off season." The more Dior's star gained ascendancy, the more Chanel's sank into obscurity.

Still, slowly, the conviction grew within Chanel that the time was approaching when women would be seized by a furious desire to throw off those waist cinchers, padded bras, heavy skirts, and stiffened jackets. Astonishingly, she even judged the right moment. By 1953 Gabrielle had made her decision and now set to work, with the idea of reopening her salon the following year. She was more than seventy years old.

△ Gabrielle Chanel, who ten years later would find a new fountain of youth in her work, returned to Paris a cruelly changed woman. In her little black bolero and utterly plain skirt, she seemed almost provincial. All that remained from the Chanel of yore was the obvious and undeniable severity of her taste.

▷ The Chanel "look." *Vogue*, 1954.

A controversial reopening

On February 5, 1954, the mood in the Rue Cambon
prior to the opening of Coco Chanel's first postwar collection resembled that of a courtroom in the final minutes before a verdict. A throng of journalists from Italy,
Germany, the United States, and England had filled the
front-row seats immediately adjacent to those taken by
the French press, and together all those women constituted a kind of tribunal.

But where was the defendant? Many of her old clients
had come to see Chanel, who, however, remained in her
favorite place, hidden away and invisible at the top of
the stairs, seated on the final step where the mirrors
permitted her to see everything without being
seen. She had consciously chosen the fifth day of
the month, for five had been her lucky number
ever since 1921, when she had given it to Chanel
No. 5, the perfume of perfumes and the founda-
tion upon which her prodigious fortune had been
built over the years (amounting to some $15 mil-
lion, if one can believe the figures published by
Time in 1971).

This precaution, however, did nothing to change
the verdict of the critics, who voted for capital pun-
ishment. One writer, Michel Déon, now a member of
the French Academy, attended that memorable
reopening at the side of Chanel. He recalled it in an
article published in *Les Nouvelles littéraires*: "The
French press were atrocious in their vulgarity, mean-
ness, and stupidity. They drubbed away at her age,
assuring everyone that she had learned nothing in
fifteen years of silence. We watched the mannequins file by in icy silence."

The headlines of the daily papers had a field day,
outdoing one another in their mockery. *Combat*:
"At Chanel's it's Fouilly-les-Oies" (meaning "way
out in the sticks"); *L'Aurore*: "A melancholy retro-
spective." The English dailies were hardly less
ferocious. "A fiasco," was how the *Daily Mail* began
its story. And if anything hurt Gabrielle, it was,
undoubtedly, the brusque and violent public contempt displayed by her English friends.

The Chanel "look" takes to the street

1954: The day after what the English-language press called a "comeback," Chanel's ability was doubted, and in the final analysis, her reopening had to be written off as a devastating loss. Moreover, the designer herself agreed that after fifteen years of inactivity she had lost her touch. Still worse was the anxiety felt by her business associates, who feared that the negative publicity might affect the sales of the Chanel perfumes.

It took Coco a year to regain her full powers, but even sooner the signs of a rapid recovery began to appear in the United States. Contrary to all expectations, the dresses presented at the reopening—those dresses which had been so severely criticized by the press that the clothing manufacturers were kicking themselves for having counted on the prestige of the Chanel name— were in fact selling better than anyone had imagined they might. New York's Seventh Avenue looked on with unbelieving eyes.

△ The fervent support of the popular magazines, and especially the weekly *Elle*.

▷ The Chanel "look," *Vogue*, 1954.

The reconquest of an empire

At the second collection presented by Chanel, *Life*, then the most widely read of all American magazines, took up the case of that very elderly lady who, after a struggle, had regained the premier position in the haute couture market. *Life* agreed that the celebrated couturière had miscalculated when she made her precipitate return, but so great had her influence already become that Chanel seemed to have initiated less a fashion than a revolution.

When asked to explain her victory, Chanel put it very simply: "A garment must be logical." And this was what she aimed for. In her view, the creations of *ces messieurs*—by which she meant her male competitors—were the very opposite of logical: "Ah no, definitely no, men were not meant to dress women." But she allowed men a role, even a determining one: it was them that women had to please.

Life began anew for Chanel. In New York the buyers along Seventh Avenue were once again calling her Coco, for the very good reason that American women could not get enough of the designer's neat little suits. In France the battle had been tough, but, for the second time in her long career, Gabrielle Chanel had changed the way women dressed and made her style dominant even in the street.

◁ A famous photograph by Irving Penn, a great master, in *Vogue*, 1960. Allure in the Chanel manner, elegance with comfort, true style, the reflection of an era.

Backstage

Once she had regained her primacy, Chanel reigned over couture, from her seventy-ninth year to her eighty-eighth, a solitary figure, respected, proud, and always tyrannical. She lived only for her work, and the passion that she brought to it was the secret of her appeal, an elixir washing away the bitterness of exile and forced inactivity.

Throughout the final days and nights prior to the first showing of each collection, the great designer had the sample dresses brought from the workrooms by the tailors and forewomen so that she could inspect them one by one. This took place in the vast mirror-lined salon where the public would crowd in on opening day. A few carefully chosen intimates were allowed to attend Gabrielle Chanel during these exhausting nights, but in silence and from a distance. The mannequins would come forth from the secrecy of the atelier—tall, ambulatory figures—and make their appearance with all the submissiveness of conscripts. They had to endure interminable fittings without uttering a syllable, knowing only too well that Chanel would have remained deaf to their protests, deaf also to their fatigue and that of the tailors.

△ On the eve of an opening, endless fittings. Photographs by Kirkland, 1962.

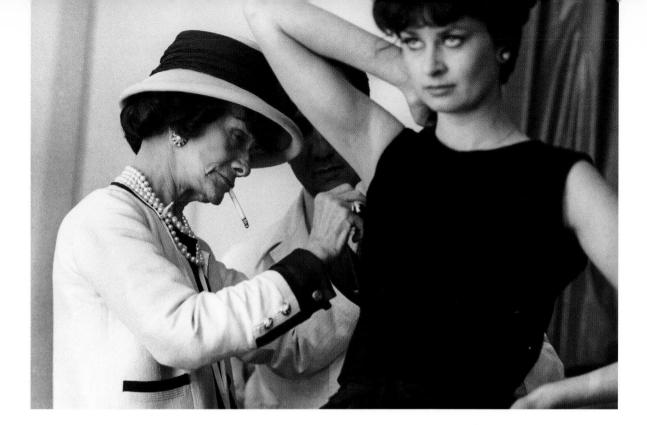

△ Gabrielle Chanel and her mannequins at work.

Again and again Chanel undid a jacket, cutting the stitches of an armhole, which she would then redo right on the mannequin, using pins to reposition it point by point, all stuck in with an almost demonic thrust. All the while she remained resolutely indifferent to everything but the creative process, a process that slowly was leading toward perfection. Her face tense, Coco scrutinized the work and, spotting a suspected bulge, seized upon the defect with fingers like talons. She would smooth and shape the material, because the flaw had to be eliminated. Finally satisfied, she would sit down, all but fainting with exhaustion. After taking a swallow of water, she might well say abruptly to a friend there: "Whatever are you looking at?" Then on to the next fitting. At last, her associates had to give up and leave her alone, well past midnight and still struggling, sometimes as humble and touching as an old artisan, but often aggressive, sure of herself, and restless, armed as she was with her long and powerful scissors, which she carried either at her belt like a sword, or around her neck like some mysterious order of knighthood.

The rite

The place was vast and seemed in no way commercial, enhanced as it was with tall windows, the teasing reflections of mirror-glazed panels, and the array of Coromandel screens that, opened out, stood around a stage, forming a sort of little theatre.

Arranged upon chairs were trays filled with necklaces, flowers, brooches, chains, and belts—embellishments ready to be selected but only in the final stage, after all the fittings of the sample dress had been finished. The moment the person in charge of accessories made a discreet appearance, the signal had come that the final touch would be applied.

△ Chanel rather liked her friendships with stage ladies. Visconti introduced Chanel to Romy Schneider, who landed in Paris a mixture of child and star. Visconti, playing Svengali, was testing her abilities through the tragedy *Dommage qu'elle soit une p . . . .* In this grand and sinister production Romy was already giving the lie to those who predicted that she would forever remain a prisoner of Sissy's Viennese mannerisms. But Chanel, who had a keen admiration for Romy Schneider, said: "She is famous before she has even started."

Then Chanel, with both hands, took the hat extended to her—more often than not a variation upon her favorite theme, the straw boater she had begun with a half-century earlier, the success of which had launched her even as she remained merely the clandestine love, the anonymous mistress of Étienne Balsan. She placed it on the head of the mannequin, pulling the form straight down and then making certain it sat securely upon the brow, and the whole occasion assumed the quality of a sacred rite. Then came the moment when, her creation having been refined, corrected, and concluded, Chanel—with that movement of a painter before her easel—stood back to see the fruits of her labor, all the while talking to herself: "Now . . . there you are . . . it's not so tacky, is it? Not too bad, don't you think? So go ahead!" This authorized the mannequin to take the ultimate pose on the podium between the Coromandel screens, for a viewing there just in case. . . . And if no alarm sounded, if she was not assaulted by a peremptory voice, the mannequin disappeared into the wings. The fitting was over.

The *défilé*

The press showing took place without flowers or music. Nothing written either, no printed statement placed on chairs so as to reveal the secret intentions of the designer, whose work they were about to judge. No program, no lyrical preface, for the simple reason that the mistress of this house had a horror of that sort of thing. She heaped sarcasm on all her rivals who resorted to what she dismissed as *la poésie couturière*. Moreover, she had been the first to abandon the practice of giving names to her dresses. The mannequins came out from the dressing room looking absolutely calm. They made their appearance in a paddock of mirrors, without winking, without provocative hip swings, and without dancing or smiling. Seated all in a row, the major clients were the first to judge. Afterwards came the reporters' turn. The mannequins walked down the line—made their *défilé*—carrying a placard marked with a number, "like jockeys astride their own horses," wrote Jean Cocteau; "provided with a registration number, like convicts," said Paul Morand. Chanel's view: "Couture is not theatre, and fashion is not an art; it's a craft."

▷△ 1956: Two Chanel classics, one a black suit with a white lining and blouse; the other a dress in black voile, whose simplicity and grace would seduce Alain Resnais, the director of *L'Année dernière à Marienbad* (1961). The film's star, Delphine Seyrig, made the Chanel style her own. The two photographs seen here are by Frances MacLaughlin for *Vogue*.

◁◁ After observing Chanel, as she stood at the top of her stairs and followed the *défilé* of her models, Maurice Sachs wrote in *La Décade de l'illusion*: "She was a General, one of the young Generals during the [Napoleonic] Empire, seized by the will to dominate."

The gestures and movements of life

Invention, talent, perfectionism, perseverance, and a vast capacity for hard work—none of it suffices to explain the power that Chanel had over women, fashion, and the artists of her time, nor why that power was so absolute. She had, it is true, a sacred account to settle with society, and possessed the "kind of solid appetite for vengeance that revolutions are made of," as Morand so rightly said. But even this cannot entirely explain or significantly clarify the mystery of such power, especially if at some moment in her career, after this had been crowned with success, the spirit of revenge subsided. Actually, it never did. On the contrary, the feeling became, if anything, more determined each time she detected in her midst some desire for a return to the past. She hated everything that, by reducing women to the status of objects, had for so long inhibited their ability to keep pace with men. Throwing off the shackles was her key obsession and her fixed objective.

It thus became essential that a skirt and jacket serve and, if possible, encourage the movements and gestures

△ Photograph by Irving Penn published in the September 1962 issue of French *Vogue*.

366

of modern life: walking, running, sudden sitting down and getting up. She condemned without appeal and with utter ferocity anything that seemed to favor the taste of another time. That a couturier should have recourse to whalebones, corsets, and petticoats was enough to make her explode with rage: "Was he mad, this man? Was he making fun of women? How, dressed in 'that thing,' could they come and go, live or anything? . . ." Live! Here was the need that gave birth to the Chanel style, the style that was her sole pride: "I don't like people talking about the Chanel fashion," she said. "Chanel—above all else, is a style. Fashion, you see, goes out of fashion. Style never."

△ A pink suit with a tragic initiation, worn by Jacqueline Kennedy during her trip to Dallas in November 1963.

△◁ Photograph by William Klein published in the October 1960 issue of French *Vogue*.

An interior for living

Gabrielle Chanel's apartment in the Rue Cambon was like a Baroque mirage set within the rigorous geometry of her commercial premises. The ateliers were above and the public salons below. Sandwiched in between, her private domain and the mystery of her three rooms evoked a certain period in a variety of ways. They gave on to the same stairway used by both clients and staff. At the end of the day, flocks of seamstresses scattered down the steps from the workrooms and took joyous flight like so many sparrows, whereas during the hours of their employment they could be seen trotting from floor to floor, smock-clad urchins and busy little bodies, their outstretched arms laden with strange forms concealed under covers. Such was the scene just outside the door leading to the

△ As famous as the celebrated staircase was the harmony of Chanel's private salon. On a deep-piled carpet in a "beaten earth" color or on a sofa covered in Havana buckskin, magical in its comfort— here one could sometimes find Chanel stretched out and reading after a harassing day, possibly asleep, or sitting as upright as the letter "I," struggling to resist fatigue, impatient and eager to plunge into one of those torrential monologues that with her passed for conversation. Photo by Robert Doisneau.

apartment where reigned the woman whom the entire house knew simply as "Mademoiselle."

The painter José-Maria Sert had advised Chanel on her first acquisitions, which were made in 1921, the period when the full flowering of her business permitted Gabrielle to "get into her own furniture." It was through this artist that the newly successful couturière learned to appreciate rare objects, beautiful mirrors, gilded wood, screens such as she had never seen before—her first Coromandels—and through him that she learned to mix periods and styles. The influence of Sert proved so tenacious that long afterward, even though she had meanwhile become sufficiently informed about everything concerning the decorative arts to dispense with an advisor, Chanel continued to be haunted by the spirit of the Ballets Russes. The interiors in which she lived would retain to the end of her life the indelible stamp of the Bakst era.

Located at 31, rue Cambon, right above her boutique and public salons, the private apartment of Chanel was photographed by Robert Doisneau around 1954.

△ Chanel, in her *art de vivre*, professed a sovereign disdain for trends and practices, an attitude fully reflected in the disposition of her private salon, where nothing conformed to an established order. Here, in this place of refuge, Gabrielle could enter into a tête-à-tête with the likes of Jeanne Moreau, whom the hostess called "the incomparable." Photograph by Giancarlo Botti.

The shelves in Chanel's library were made of simple, hastily painted planks in the midst of which hung, as if enshrined, her magnificent mirrors. Gilded bronze sculptures, of different periods and various origins, served as bookends. This insistence upon placing books of every kind, all superbly bound, within arm's reach was Chanel's way of expressing contempt for bibliophiles, book lovers who kept their treasures under glass and often under lock and key.

◁ Gabrielle Chanel, captured by Henri Cartier-Bresson in 1964.

▷ Chanel took great pride in her stable of mannequins, whom she regarded as her best public. Moreover, she never engaged extra ones at collection time. The Chanel stable resembled none other. Whereas the postwar period brought the era of the mannequin-star—equipped with, in addition to her beauty, a given name or simply a surname, such as Victoire, Kouka, Praline, or Bettina—Chanel, beginning in 1955, one year after her comeback, built herself a stable of young women-about-town, often well-born, choosing them as much for their personality as for their physical loveliness. Here we see, on either side of "Mademoiselle," Ghislaine Arsac, Marie-Hélène Arnaud, Suzy Parker, Odile de Croy, Paule Rizzo, Mimi d'Arcangues, Nicole Francomme, and Paule de Mérindol.

Altogether, it consisted of three rooms whose walls were covered with a simple copper-gold paper, which, however, was scarcely visible behind lacquered Coromandel screens, books, and carved wood. As for the eternally traveling screens, those panels always subject to change, it was their obvious movability that created the impression of a royal encampment. By the very sumptuousness of these assembled pieces, Chanel made it evident that she had become the equal of the very rich, but by the sovereign casualness of their placement, without protection of any sort, she managed to indicate that she attached no importance to their monetary value and that they were there solely for her pleasure.

Consecration on Broadway

1970: Katharine Hepburn in the role of Mademoiselle Chanel. This was big news in the world of New York show biz, for it concerned a musical comedy starring a great actress who had never before sung or danced. For years, the producer Fred Brisson had been trying to persuade Chanel to let him do a play based upon her life, and now she had given her consent. Broadway was to take advantage of the Chanel myth. None other than the *My Fair Lady* team was to prepare the show: Alan Jay Lerner for the lyrics and Sir Cecil Beaton for the 250 costumes. *Coco* became the most expensive production ever to appear on Broadway. Two weeks before opening night, some $1.5 million in tickets had been sold. Despite a poor critical reception, *Coco* played to full houses. The fabled Hepburn, who, like Chanel, seemed to defy the passage of time, transcended her sixty years to achieve a personal triumph.

△ ▷ Katharine Hepburn in the title role of *Coco*. Beaton's costumes simply paraphrased the Chanel style, perhaps a bit heavy-handedly. Coco herself refused all comment, allowing her silence to speak volumes. At the last minute she declined to attend the opening. Among her aphorisms we discover the following: "Failed innovation is painful; revival of it is sinister."

Maxims penned by Chanel.
What she thought about life,
love, women, and her profession.

Chanelisms—the maxims attributed to Chanel (see page 377) — appeared in many magazines in France and abroad, especially in England, Germany, and Italy. The style and tone of the sayings, their unmistakable quality, their economy, never fail to impress and, with the passage of time, have left little doubt about their authenticity. But was Chanel their actual author? A review of her correspondence reveals a vast discrepancy between the clumsiness of Chanel the letter-writer and the talent of Chanel as a composer of maxims.

A letter written to Chanel by her friend the poet Pierre Reverdy, clarifies the mystery beyond all argument. No question about it, Gabrielle regularly sought his advice. Also not to be doubted is the fact that Reverdy procured examples that she could follow: *Les Caractères* of La Bruyère and the famous *Sentences et Maximes* of La Rochefoucauld. "Pick them up from time to time," he wrote, "a few each evening." It is also certain that in her eagerness to ease the material existence of one of France's greatest and least appreciated writers, Chanel proposed that he join her as a paid collaborator. Thus, after correcting the handful of aphorisms that Chanel wrote, exclusively about her métier, Reverdy added to this collection of "Chanelisms" a series of thoughts of a more general nature, some touching on life and taste and others on allure and love.

▷ In Chanel's private salon, a large angel in gilded wood set against a background of Coromandel screens.

It is said that women dress for other women, and out of a spirit of competition. This is true. But if there were no longer any men, women would no longer dress at all.

"Good taste" ruins certain real values of the spirit: taste itself, for instance.

Fashion has two purposes: comfort and love. Beauty comes when fashion succeeds.

An elegant woman should be able to do her marketing without making housewives laugh. Those who laugh are always right.

Costume designers work with a pencil: it is art. Couturiers with scissors and pins: it is a news item.

Sem said to me, concerning some jewelry that I had designed: "At last we imitate the fake." How right he was. It is impossible to wear lots of real jewels unless there are women who wear lots of fake ones.

It is in paintings or in family albums that traces of true fashion are to be found.

Coquetry, it's a triumph of the spirit over the senses.

True generosity means accepting ingratitude.

The time comes when one can do nothing further to a work; this is when it has reached its worst.

Comfort has forms. Love has colors. A skirt is made for crossing the legs and an armhole for crossing the arms.

Fashion is at once both caterpillar and butterfly. Be a caterpillar by day and a butterfly by night. Nothing could be more comfortable than a caterpillar and nothing more made for love than a butterfly. There must be dresses that crawl and dresses that fly. The butterfly does not go to market, and the caterpillar does not go to a ball.

To disguise oneself is charming: to have oneself disguised is sad.

Fashion does not exist unless it goes down into the streets. The fashion that remains in the salons has no more significance than a costume ball.

Adornment, what a science! Beauty, what a weapon! Modesty, what elegance!

For a woman, to deceive makes only one kind of sense: that of the senses.

Make the dress first, not the embellishment.

A dress is not a dressing. It is made to be worn. One wears clothes with the shoulders. A dress should hang from the shoulders.

One day I heard an old seamstress saying to a young seamstress: "Never a button without a buttonhole." This simple and admirable statement could serve as a motto for couturiers and also for architects, musicians, and painters.

A failed innovation is painful: revival of it is sinister.

Fashion should slip out of your hands. The very idea of protecting the seasonal arts is childish. One should not bother to protect that which dies the minute it is born.

A beautiful dress may look beautiful on a hanger, but that means nothing. It must be seen on the shoulders, with the movement of the arms, the legs, and the waist.

Our houses are our prisons: let us learn how to liberate ourselves in the way we arrange them.

One can get used to ugliness, but never to negligence.

Fashion is always a reflection of its own time, but we forget this if it is stupid.

Nature gives you the face you have at twenty; life shapes the face you have at thirty; but at fifty, you get the face you deserve.

If you were born without wings, do nothing to prevent their growing.

Luxury is a necessity that begins where necessity ends.

Après-Chanel has a name: Karl Lagerfeld

Chanel prepared no successor, and to take over from that legendary woman, whose impact on the world of fashion had been incalculable, entailed a daunting number of risks. In 1983, twelve years after the death of Gabrielle Chanel, Karl Lagerfeld assumed the perilous task of becoming artistic director of an enterprise that had depended entirely upon the talent of its founder. With his own style, means, and creative abilities, with his own very considerable reputation, Karl Lagerfeld set about not only to keep alive the name, work, and especially the elegance and refinement of a personality from the past but also to make them flourish. A big gamble, but Lagerfeld won it. Endlessly copying Chanel and her ideas would have been the worst possible solution. To continue creating pastiches or repeatedly issuing models "in the manner of" would have been almost as deadly an outcome.

The answer was to innovate. Like Chanel, Karl Lagerfeld knew how to be of his own time; moreover, he understood how to be himself without making a fetish of it. Here and there, when moved to do so, Lagerfeld, in each of his collections for Chanel, paid tribute to the spirit of the Grande Mademoiselle, sometimes with irony and a light touch, sometimes with respect and admiration, always by way of some witty quotation. Never did Lagerfeld play the copyist. Rather, he proceeds like a great composer working through a set of variations on a given theme—a theme with the name Chanel.

△ Self-portrait by Karl Lagerfeld.

◁ A sketch by Karl Lagerfeld portraying Gabrielle Chanel. As a child, "King Karl," as the fashion world calls him, hoped to become a portrait painter. Ever since he lives with a pencil in hand, sketching as easily as he breathes.

▷ An accomplished photographer, Lagerfeld took this picture of one of his creations for the prêt-à-porter collection launched in the 2002/2003 fall/winter season.

Index

Photographic credits

Endpapers: © Chanel; **p. 2:** © Bridgeman Art Library; **p. 4:** © Adagp, 2004; **p. 6:** © Adagp, 2004; **p. 7:** Patrimoine Photographique, Paris; **p. 8:** © Adagp, 2004; **p. 12:** © Rancurel; **p. 13 above:** Hyde/RMN/Musée des Arts et Traditions Populaires, Paris; **pp. 13 bottom and 14 left:** © Rancure; **p. 14 right:** © Doisneau/Rapho; **p. 15:** © Rancurel; **p. 16:** © Blanchard/Saumur; **p. 17 left:** © Blanchard/Saumur ; **p. 17 right:** © Simone Brousse; **p. 19:** © Blanchard/Saumur; **p. 20:** private collection; **p. 21 above:** © Doisneau/Rapho; **p. 21 below:** © Atget/Bibliothèque Nationale de France, Paris; **p. 22:** © private collection E. C.-R.; **p. 24 above:** Bridgeman Art Library; **p. 24 below:** © P.H. Martinez; **p. 25 above:** © private collection E. C.-R.; **p. 25 below left:** © Camille Gomard; **p. 25 below right:** © private collection E. C.-R.; **p. 26 left:** Roger-Viollet; **p. 26 right:** © Henriette Dussourd; **p. 27:** Bossi; **p. 28 above right:** Jean-Charles Varennes; **p. 28 below left:** Genermont/Rancurel; **p. 28 below right:** Jacques Dubois; **p. 29 left and below right:** © private collection E. C.-R.; **p. 29 above right:** Jean-Charles Varennes; **p. 30 left:** Clément/Archives Départementales de l'Allier; **p. 30 right:** Bibliothèque Historique de la Ville de Paris; **p. 31:** Bibliothèque de l'Opéra, Paris; **p. 32:** Musée Bargouin, Clermont-Ferrand; **p. 33:** Adrien Eche; **p. 34:** Bibliothèque de l'Opéra, Paris; **p. 35:** H.G. Ibels, drawing for *Les Demi-Cabots de Montorgueil*, Bibliothèque Nationale de France, Paris; **p. 36:** Maurice Danière; **p. 37:** © private collection E. C.-R.; **p. 38:** Bibliothèque de l'Opéra, Paris; **p. 39:** Jean-Charles Varennes ; **pp. 40–41:** Bibliothèque de l'Opéra, Paris; **pp. 42–44:** © private collection E. C.-R.; **pp. 45–47:** **p. 48 left:** © private collection E. C.-R.; **p. 48 right:** Musée du Costume, Paris; **p. 49 :** © private collection E. C.-R.; **p. 50:** Bibliothèque Nationale de France, Paris; **p. 52:** Sirot-Angel; **p. 53:** Bridgeman Art Library; **p. 54–57:** © private collection E. C.-R.; **p. 58:** Roxane Debuisson; **p. 59:** Archives Photographiques, Paris; **p. 60 above:** © private collection E. C.-R.; **p. 60 below:** Coursaget; **p. 61 above left:** Sirot-Angel; **p. 61 above right:** Centre de Documentation du Costume, Paris; **p. 61 right:** © private collection E. C.-R.; **p. 62 left:** Sirot-Angel; **p. 62 right:** Musée du Costume, Paris; **pp. 63–65:** © private collection E. C.-R.; **p. 66:** private collection; **p. 67 left:** Roger-Viollet; **p. 67 right:** Archives Photographiques, Paris; **p. 68:** Bridgeman Art Library; **p. 69 left:** Roger-Viollet; **p. 69 right:** Bibliothèque de l'Arsenal, Paris; **p. 70:** © private collection E. C.-R.; **p. 71 above left:** Studio Vogue; **p. 71 below right:** © private collection E. C.-R.; **p. 72:** Studio Vogue; **p. 73 above left:** © private collection E. C.-R.; **p. 73 below left:** © private collection E. C.-R.; **p. 73 right:** © private collection E. C.-R.; **p. 74:** © private collection E. C.-R.; **p. 75:** © private collection E. C.-R.; **p. 76:** Seeberger; **p. 77:** Sirot Angel; **pp. 78–81:** © private collection E. C.-R.; **p. 82:** Studio Vogue; **p. 83:** © private collection E. C.-R.; **p. 84:** D.R.; **p. 85:** Studio Vogue; **pp. 86–87:** © private collection E. C.-R.; **p. 88:** Keystone; **p. 89:** Bridgeman Art Library; **p. 90 left and right:** *Comœdia*; **p. 91 left:** Talbot photo published in *Les Modes*, Bibliothèque Nationale de France, Paris; **p. 91 right:** Rancurel; **p. 92 above left and right:** drawings published in *Les Années folles*, Guilleminault, Denoël, 1958; **p. 92 above center:** drawing published in *Les Modes*, 1912, Bibliothèque Nationale de France, Paris ; **p. 92 below:** Bridgeman Art Library; **p. 93 left:** photo published in *Les Modes*, 1912, Bibliothèque Nationale de France, Paris; **p. 93 right:** Seeberger; **p. 94:** Seeberger, Bibliothèque Nationale de France, Paris; **p. 95 above:** © private collection E. C.-R.; **p. 95 below:** © private collection E. C.-R.; **p. 96:** D.R.; **p. 98:** Marcel Jouhandeau; **p. 99 left:** D.R.; **p. 99 right:** Michel Remy-Bieth; **p. 100:** Josette Gris; **p. 101:** Fondation Maeght/Succession Picasso; **p. 102:** AKG; **p. 103:** Pierrette Gargallo; **p. 104:** Archives *Match*; **p. 106:** © Adagp, 2004; **p. 108:** Sirot-Angel; **p. 109:** © private collection E. C.-R.; **p. 110–111:** Chennebenoistv; **p. 112:** © private collection E. C.-R.; **pp. 113–114:** © private collection E. C.-R.; **pp. 115–117:** © Adagp, 2004; **pp. 118–119:** © private collection E. C.-R.; **p. 120 left:** © private collection E. C.-R.; **p. 120 right:** Sirot-Angel; **p. 121:** Bridgeman Art Library; **p. 122:** Pierre Marcel Adima; **p. 123 left:** drawing published in *Comœdia*; **p. 123 right:** © private collection E. C.-R.; **p. 124:** Sirot-Angel; **p. 125:** © AFP; **p. 126:** Keystone; **p. 127:** Roger-Viollet; **p. 128:** © *Marie-Claire*; **p. 129:** Bridgeman Art Library; **p. 130:** photo published in *Harper's Bazaar*, **p. 131:** © private collection E. C.-R.; **pp. 132–133:** Bridgeman Art Library; **p. 134:** drawing published in *Les Elégances parisiennes*, 1917; **p. 135 left:** photo published in *Fémina*, June 1917; **p. 135 right:** drawing published in *Les Elégances parisiennes*, 1917; **pp. 136–137:** © private collection E. C.-R.; **p. 138 left:** © private collection E. C.-R.; **p. 138 right:** drawing published in *Fémina*, June 1917; **p. 139 above and below:** © private collection E. C.-R.; **pp. 140–142:** © private collection E. C.-R.; **p. 143 left:** Modigliani, *Portrait de Madame Kisling*, RMN; **p. 143 right:** Marcel Jouhandeau; **pp. 144–147:** © private collection E. C.-R.; **pp. 148–149:** private collection, © Adagp, 2004; **pp. 150–151:** D.R., © Adagp, 2004; **p. 152:** D.R.; **p. 152:** © Adagp, 2004; **p. 153:** © Adagp, 2004; **p. 154:** © Adagp, 2004; **p. 155 left:** Boris Kochno; **p. 155 right:** private collection; **p. 156:** private collection; **p. 157:** private collection, © Adagp, 2004; **p. 158:** AKG, © Adagp, 2004; **p. 159:** private collection; **p. 160:** Artothek, © Adagp, 2004; **p. 161:** RMN, © Adagp, 2004; **p. 162:** Boris Kochno; **p. 163:** private collection, © Adagp, 2004; **p. 164:** Boris Kochno; **p. 165:** Bibliothèque de l'Opéra, Jean Cocteau collection, Paris, © Adagp, 2004; **pp. 166, 169:** private collection, © Adagp, 2004; **p. 170:** Roger-Viollet; **p. 171:** Boris Kochno; **p. 172:** Bibliothèque Doucet, Paris; **p. 173:** D.R.; **p. 174:** D.R.; **p. 175:** Michel Rémy-Bieth; **p. 176:** AKG, © Adagp, 2004; **p. 177:** D.R.; **p. 178 left:** Henri de Beaumont; **p. 178 right:** D.R.; **p. 179:** private collection/Succession Picasso; **p. 180:** *Vogue*; **p. 181:** D.R.; **p. 182:** Georges Gruber-Bernstein; **p. 183:** © private collection E. C.-R.; **p. 184 left:** © Chanel; **p. 184 right:** © ADP/Archives *Le Provençal*; **p. 185:** © Chanel; **p. 186:** drawing published in *Vogue*, Paris, 1923; **p. 187:** © Adagp, 2004; **p. 188 above:** Georges Gruber-Bernstein; **p. 188 below:** *Saturday Evening Post*; **p. 189 above:** © private collection E. C.-R.; **p. 189 below left:** © private collection E. C.-R.; **p. 189 below right:** *Vogue*; **p. 190:** *Vogue*, Paris; **p. 191:** *Vogue*; **p. 192:** *Vogue*; **p. 193:** Bibliothèque de l'Opéra, Paris; **p. 194:** © Talpain; **p. 195:** Dolly Van Dongen; **pp. 196–197:** Boris Kochno; **pp. 198–199:** *Vogue*; **pp. 200–201:** private collection; **p. 202:** George Hoyningen-Huene/*Vanity Fair*, © 1934 Condé Nast Publications Inc., New York; **p. 203 left:** drawing by Drian published in *Harper's Bazaar*/Hearst Corporation, © Adagp, 2004; **p. 203 right:** *Vogue*, Paris; **p. 204 above:** D.R.; **p. 204 below left and right:** Georges Gruber-Bernstein; **p. 205 above left and right:** drawing published in *L'Illustration*/D.R.; **p. 205 below:** Boris Kochno; **p. 206 left:** Keystone; **p. 206 above and below right:** Bibliothèque de l'Opéra, Paris/Succession Picasso; **p. 207:** *The Times*, London; **p. 208:** RMN/Succession Picasso; **p. 209:** Bibliothèque de l'Opéra, Paris; **pp. 210–212:** Bibliothèque de l'Opéra, Anton Dolin collection, Paris; **p. 213:** © Desjardins; **pp. 214 and 215 left:** D.R., Costa de Beauregard; **p. 215 right:** Henri de Beaumont; **p. 216 left:** Archives Bernard Dunand; **p. 216 right:** *Vogue*, Paris; **pp. 218–219:** Archives Bernard Dunand; **p. 220:** drawing by J. Touchet published in *L'Illustration*; **p. 221:** Rue des Archives; **p. 222:** Archives de l'Académie Française, Paul Morand collection, Paris; **p. 223:** drawing by Kees van Dongen for the cover of Paul Morand's novel *Magie noire*, Édition Grasset, © Adagp, 2004; **p. 224:** Condé Nast Publication, New York; **pp. 225, 226, 227 left and right, 228, 229:** *Vogue*, Paris; **pp. 230–231:** © Doisneau/Rapho; **pp. 232–235:** © private collection E. C.-R.; **pp. 236–237:** *Vogue*; **p. 238:** *Sunday Telegraph*; **p. 239:** Henri de Beaumont; **p. 240 left and right:** Chanel-Laget; **p. 241:** Radio Times, Hulton Picture Library; **p. 242:** Bridgeman Art Library; **pp. 243–244:** © private collection E. C.-R.; **p. 245:** Boris Kochno; **p. 246:** *Sunday Telegraph*; **p. 247:** © Roger Schall; **p. 248:** Keystone; **p. 249:** photo published in *L'Illustration*; **p. 250:** D.R., © Adagp, 2004; **p. 251:** Archives de l'Académie Française, Paul Morand collection, Paris; **p. 252:** © Adagp, 2004; **p. 253:** Galerie Proscenium, © Adagp, 2004; **p. 254:** Sacha Pitoëff; **p. 255:** Costa de Beauregard; **pp. 256–257:** Henri de Beaumont; **p. 258 left and right:** Galerie Proscenium, © Adagp, 2004; **p. 259:** © Jean Roubier; **pp. 260–261:** Galerie Proscenium, © Adagp, 2004; **pp. 262–263:** Cecil B. DeMille; **p. 264:** Cinémathèque Française; **p. 265:** Academy of Motion Picture, Arts & Sciences; **pp. 266–269:** Cinémathèque Française/D.R.; **pp. 270–271:** photos published in *L'Illustration*; **p. 272:** © private collection E. C.-R.; **p. 274:** J. H. Lartigue/© Ministère de la Culture-France/AAJHL; **p. 275:** Leclère; **p. 276:** *Vogue*, Paris; **p. 277:** Boris Kochno; **p. 278:** Museum of Modern Art/Films Stills Archives; **p. 279:** *Match*; **pp. 280–281:** Cinémathèque Française; **p. 282:** © Lipnitzki-Viollet; **p. 283:**© M. Piquemal-France Match; **p. 284:** *Vogue*, Paris; **p. 285:** Henri de Beaumont; **p. 286 left and right:** Henri de Beaumont; **p. 287:** Henri de Beaumont; **p. 288:** © Chanel; **p. 289:** Denise Tual; **p. 290:** private collection; **p. 291:** Rue des Archives; **p. 292 left:** Henri de Beaumont; **p. 292 right:** *Vogue*, Paris; **p. 293:** Henri de Beaumont; **pp. 294–295:** *Vogue*; **pp. 296–297:** Seeberger, Paris; **p. 298:** Horst/*Vogue*, © 1935 Condé Nast Publications Inc., New York; **p. 299:** © Horst/Condé Nast Publications Inc., New York; **pp. 300–301:** Condé Nast Publications Inc., New York ; **p. 302:** © Lipnitzki/Roger-Viollet; **pp. 303, 304, 305 above:** © Adagp, 2004; **p. 305 below:** © private collection E. C.-R.; **p. 306 left:** © Lipnitzki/Roger-Viollet; **p. 306 right:** private collection; **p. 307:** © Lipnitzki/Roger-Viollet; **pp. 308–309:** © Roger Schall; **p. 310:** © Talpain; **p. 311:** © David Seymour/Magnum; **pp. 312–315:** Keystone; **p. 316:** Bibliothèque Nationale de France, Paris; **p. 317:** © Seeberger; **p. 318:** D.R.; **p. 319:** Bibliothèque Nationale de France, Paris; **pp. 320–321:** © Lipnitzki/Roger-Viollet; **p. 322:** © private collection E. C.-R.; **pp. 324–325:** drawing by Pagès, *Vogue* ; **p. 326–327:** © Horst; **p. 328:** *Vogue*, © Adagp, 2004; **p. 329 left:** © Roger Schall; **p. 329 right:** *Vogue*, © Adagp, 2004; **pp. 330–331:** © Cecil Beaton/Condé Nast Publications Inc., New York; **p. 332:** © Horst/Condé Nast Publications Inc., New York; **p. 333–334:** © Roger Schall; **p. 335 above and below:** © Roger Schall; **pp. 336–337:** *Vogue*, Paris; **p. 338:** © Henri Amouroux; **p. 339:** © private collection E. C.-R.; **p. 340:** Rue des Archives; **pp. 341–342:** Keystone; **p. 343:** D.R.; **pp. 344–345:** © Roger Schall; **p. 346:** © Pierre Valls; **p. 347:** © De Sazo/Rapho; **p. 348:** © Richard Avedon; **p. 349 above:** © Cartier-Bresson/Magnum; **p. 349 below:** private collection; **p. 350:** *Vogue*, Paris, © Adagp, 2004; **p. 351:** Photo Publicité Christian Dior; **p. 352:** Condé Nast Publications Inc./*Vogue*, Great Britain; **p. 353:** © AFP; **p. 354:** © Doisneau/Rapho; **p. 355:** *Vogue*, Paris; **p. 356 left and right:** © J.-F. Clair/Elle-Scoop; **p. 357:** Henry Clarke/*Vogue*, © 1954 Condé Nast Publications Inc., New York; **p. 358:** © Irving Penn/Condé Nast Publications Inc., New York; **pp. 360–361:** © Kirkland/Corbis; **p. 362:** © Botti/Gamma; **p. 364:** © Roger Schall; **p. 365 left and right:** © Frances MacLaughlin; **p. 366:** © Irving Penn/Condé Nast Publications Inc., New York; **p. 367 left:** © William Klein; **p. 367 right:** D.R.; **p. 368:** © Robert Doisneau/Rapho; **p. 369:** © Botti/Gamma; **p. 370:** © Cartier-Bresson/Magnum; **p. 371:** © Willy Rizzo; **p. 372–373:** D.R.; **p. 375:** © Roger Schall; **p. 376:** © Suzy Parker/Condé Nast Publications Inc., Paris; **p. 378 left and right:** © Karl Lagerfeld/Chanel; **p. 379:** © Karl Lagerfeld/model Karolina Kurkova/Agence Viva/Chanel.

Documents cited as © private collection E. C.-R. are subject to prior authorization.

Acknowledgments

The author thanks the House of Chanel not only for the information and advice it provided but also for access to the Chanel photographic archives.

She is grateful as well to Susan Train, the Paris bureau chief of Condé Nast Publications, Inc., for her generous support of this project, and to Dominique Paulvé for her help with illustrations. Similarly, she acknowledges anew the contributions made by numerous people to the original edition, published in 1979:

M. Pierre-Marcel ADEMA
M. Henri AMOUROUX
Mme Étienne BALSAN
Sir Cecil BEATON
Comte Henri de BEAUMONT
M. Pierre BERTIN
Mme Sibylle BILLOT
M. Georges BORCHARDT
Mme Paule de BROGLIE
Mme Marie-Hélène CAMUS
M. Jean CARDOSI
M. David CHIERICHETTI
M. Jérôme CLEMENT
Comtesse Amédée COSTA de BEAUREGARD
Mme Hélène DESSOFFY
M. Robert DOISNEAU

M. Anton DOLIN
Mme Gabrielle DORZIAT
M. Frantz DOUCHNITZ
Mme Henriette DUSSOURD
Mme Raymonde FRAISSE
M. Philippe GARNER
M. Benno GRAZIANI
Mme Georges GRUBER-BERNSTEIN
M. Nicolas de GUNZBURG
Mme Martine KAHANE
M. Boris KOCHNO
M. Jacques Henri LARTIGUE
Mme Gaston LECLERE
M. Pierre LÉVY
M. Marvin LYONS
M. Aimé MAEGHT

M. Ralph MEIMA
M. Hervé MILLE
M. Jean-Yves MOCK
Baron Ferréol de NEXON
Vicomte Charles de NOAILLES
M. Michel REMY-BIETH
M. André ROSSEL
M. Antoine SALOMON
M. Henri SAUGUET
Mme Romy SCHNEIDER
Mme SELTEN-RICH
M. Roger THÉROND
Mme Denise TUAL
Mme Jeanine WARNOD
Condé Nast Publications, Paris and New York

Originally published in French as *Le Temps Chanel* by Éditions de la Martinière, Paris and Éditions Grasset and Fasquelle, Paris.

First published in the United States of America in 2005 by
The Vendome Press
1334 York Avenue
New York, NY 10021

Copyright © 2004 Éditions de la Martinière
Copyright © 2004 Éditions Grasset and Fasquelle
English translation copyright © 1981 & 2005 The Vendome Press

ISBN: 0-86565-159-0

Translation from the French: Daniel Wheeler
Picture research: Nathalie Chapuis
Design and layout: Élisabeth Ferté
Editorial coordination for the French edition: Anne de Marnhac

Library of Congress Cataloging-in-Publication Data

Charles-Roux, Edmonde.
  [Le temps Chanel. English]
  Chanel and her world : friends, fashion, and fame / Edmonde Charles-Roux.-- Rev. and expanded
      p. cm.
  Includes bibliographical references and index.
  ISBN 0-86565-159-0 (hardcover : alk. paper)
  1. Chanel, Coco, 1883-1971. 2. Fashion designers--France--Biography. 3. Women fashion designers--France--Biography. 4. Fashion desi-gners--France--Pictorial works. 5. Women fashion designers--France--Pictorial works. 6. France--Social life and customs--20th century--Pictorial works. I. Title.
  TT505.C45C4713 2005
  746.9'2'092--dc22

                          2004019368

Printed in China
Second printing